Winner-Takes-All

Winner-Takes-All

THE SECRET HISTORY OF THE ELECTORAL COLLEGE

James Moyer

Note

This book is devoted to all voters.

The book is intended to be a nonpartisan discussion of how elections for presidential electors work. It mentions concrete partisan events, but does so simply to illustrate to voters of any persuasion what is happening.

Whether this book does or does not influence your vote in this election or any future one is up to you. You are the citizen; it is your vote.

Table of Contents

Figures

CHAPTER 1

The Basics

Every four years in November, America's greatest democratic event occurs.

It is the election of the 538 presidential electors.[1]

That is Stage One, where American voters *create the composition* of the Electoral College.

In Stage Two, in December of the election year, the 538 electors then elect the president.

What makes Stage One confusing is it's not obvious that voters are electing the electors.

What makes Stage Two confusing is that what any one elector is capable of doing is a function of the other 537.

---

[1] Technically, two of Maine's and two of Nebraska's electors aren't elected. So it's more accurate to say 534. Maine and Nebraska are covered later.

CHAPTER 2

Where Do Presidential Electors Come From?

GENERALLY THE STATE POLITICAL PARTIES nominate their candidates for presidential elector at their respective state conventions.

In the case of minor parties or independent tickets, candidates for presidential elector are nominated when the presidential ticket candidacy paperwork is submitted.

Political parties typically name party loyalists to be their electors. Sometimes they are political officials, party volunteers, or large donors.

These lists have to be turned into state election official's offices by August or September. The lists of candidates for presidential elector are then compiled for the November election.

The Hidden Multiplier: How Voters Elect Presidential Electors

How voters elect the Presidential Electors is a confusing topic because of the way that it is presented in the media and on the ballots.

Regarding the forty-nine "winner-takes-all" states (which includes Washington, DC), people believe that they are casting a "popular vote" and that the presidential ticket, which wins the plurality of a state's popular vote, will take all of the state's electors.

This is not how this works in any state. In fact, this is backward.

In reality, voters in the forty-nine states and DC are voting *directly* for presidential electors.

The 2016 Colorado ballot, shown here, is correctly labeled, and voters are voting for the presidential electors.

What is confusing/weird is that *none* of the people listed on the 2016 Colorado ballot are presidential electors.

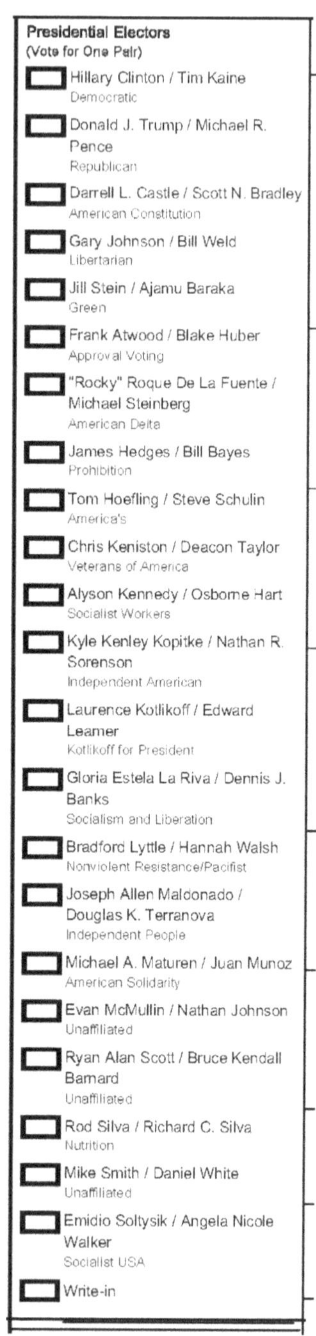

Figure 3.1 The 2016 Colorado Ballot

The 2016 Colorado ballot featured twenty-two presidential tickets as well as a write-in space.[2]

For simplicity, let's focus on just the top four vote-receiving presidential tickets.

Presidential Ticket vote count, Top 4, Colorado 2016	
Clinton/Kaine (D)	1,338,870
Trump/Pence (R)	1,202,484
Johnson/Weld (L)	144,121
Stein/Baraka (G)	38.437

Figure 3.2 2016 Colorado Presidential ticket vote count, top 4 tickets

Colorado has nine electoral seats. This means each of the four Presidential tickets listed above has nine elector candidates who are nominated by their respective political parties.

When a Colorado voter votes for any of the Presidential tickets listed above, *they are casting nine votes simultaneously*—one for each of the nine elector candidates.

The above therefore is not the true result of the 2016 election. The true result is below.

---

[2] 2016 Colorado sample ballot, Kiowa County. Colorado's ballot access laws, allowing those many candidates on the ballot, is particularly generous and certainly a national model. Few Americans will see these many choices. Some will only have two choices. If that is your state, it is because the political powers of your state prefer it that way.

Democratic Electors	Vote Totals	Republican Electors	Vote Totals	Libertarian Electors	Vote Totals	Green Electors	Vote Totals
Micheal Baca	1,338,870	Jim O'Dell	1,202,484	Steven Gallant	144,121	Andrea Merida	38,437
Terry Phillips	1,338,870	Robert Blaha	1,202,484	Joseph Thompson	144,121	Amanda Trujillo	38,437
Mary Beth Corsentino	1,338,870	Laurel Imer	1,202,484	Kevin Gulbranson	144,121	Angela Humphrey	38,437
Jerad Sutton	1,338,870	Edward Stephen Barlock	1,202,484	Michele Poague	144,121	Jason Justice	38,437
Robert Nemanich	1,338,870	Charlie McNeil	1,202,484	Eva F. Kosinski	144,121	Lora Reuther	38,437
Amy Drayer	1,338,870	Bill Cagle	1,202,484	Kim Tavendale	144,121	Joseph Scardetta	38,437
Ann Knollman	1,338,870	Pete Coors	1,202,484	Michael Stapleton	144,121	Annamarie Martinez	38,437
Rollie Heath	1,338,870	Steve House	1,202,484	Mike Spalding	144,121	Dustin Tebbetts-Fiore	38,437
Polly Baca	1,338,870	Eileen Milzcik	1,202,484	Ken Wyble	144,121	Brianna Friend	38,437

Figure 3.3 The true election results of the 2016 Colorado Presidential Elector election, top 4 tickets

In the simplified count shown here, there are thirty-six presidential elector candidates. There are nine elector seats available. The top nine will be seated as elected officials. Who are the top nine? The electors nominated by the Democratic party, since each received 1,338,870 votes.

This is what happens in any of the forty-nine "winner-takes-all" states and DC. Voters are casting multiple votes simultaneously equal to the amount of electors that state has.

A Vermont voter casts three votes simultaneously.

An Ohio voter casts eighteen votes simultaneously.

A California voter casts fifty-five votes simultaneously.

This book calls this effect "the hidden multiplier." Voters think they are casting only one vote, when in reality, in the forty-nine "winner-takes-all" jurisdictions, they are casting at least three and as many as fifty-five.

Perhaps one might wonder: If a Colorado voter is casting multiple votes simultaneously, why can't the voter split their nine votes between different presidential tickets?

In fact, Colorado voters could split their ballots until 1940.

FOR PRESIDENTIAL ELECTORS		Mark in this Column
	(Vote for Six)	
REPUBLICAN PARTY For President of the United States **Herbert Hoover** For Vice-President of the United States **Charles Curtis**	MRS. LEONARD E. ANDERSON	
	FRANK L. BIRNEY	
	CHARLES HAYDEN	
	CHARLES N. JACKSON	
	CHARLES ALFRED JOHNSON	
	JESSE F. McDONALD	
DEMOCRATIC PARTY For President of the United States **Alfred E. Smith** For Vice-President of the United States **Joseph T. Robinson**	TYSON S. DINES	
	MRS. ELEANOR GOSS	
	LAFAYETTE M. HUGHES	
	MILES G. SAUNDERS	
	GUY V. STERNBERG	
	JESSE C. WILEY	
WORKERS-COMMUNIST For President of the United States **Wm. Z. Foster** For Vice-President of the United States **Benjamin Gitlow**	JAMES AYRES	
	WILLIAM DIETRICH	
	AUBREY C. LEWIS	
	GEO. J. SAUL	
	JAMES I. WHIDDEN	
	LOUIS A. ZEITLIN	
SOCIALIST PARTY For President of the United States **Norman Thomas** For Vice-President of the United States **James H. Maurer**	THOMAS J. BROWN	
	CLAUD A. BUSHNELL	
	JEROME MORGAN	
	ALFRED E. SMITH	
	CHANNING SWEET	
	HENRY H. SWEETLAND	
FARMER-LABOR PARTY For President of the United States **Frank Elbridge Webb** For Vice-President of the United States **Robert Lee Tillman**	GEORGE BRADY	
	W. C. FLOCKER	
	GEO. M. GILBERT	
	WM. W. HENDERSON	
	JOHN A. QUIGLEY	
	WM. P. WILLIAMS	

Figure 3.4 1928 Colorado Presidential Elector ballot

Pictured here is a 1928 Colorado sample ballot (city and county of Denver).[3]

As you can see, Colorado had six electoral votes in 1928, and voters could split those six votes as they see fit.

A table follows with the true election results of the 1928 election.[4]

Republican Electors	Vote Totals	Democratic Electors	Vote Totals	Workers-Communist Electors	Vote Totals
Anderson	252,924	Dines	132,747	Ayres	**675**
Birney	**253,872**	Goss	**133,131**	Dietrich	620
Hayden	253,583	Hughes	133,105	Lewis	537
Jackson	253,181	Saunders	132,907	Saul	458
Johnson	253,545	Sternberg	132,765	Whidden	443
McDonald	251,765	Wiley	132,101	Zeitlin	423

Socialist Electors	Vote Totals	Farmer-Labor Electors	Vote Totals
Brown	2,630	Brady	**1,092**
Bushnell	2,551	Flocker	961
Morgan	2,512	Gilbert	987
Smith	**3,472**	Henderson	999
Sweet	2,518	Quigley	949
Sweetland	2,461	Williams	1,022

Figure 3.5 1928 Colorado Presidential Elector vote totals

Numbers in bold are the highest vote total for any elector in that slate. This is what election historians use as the "popular vote" for that presidential ticket.

---

[3] November 1928 City and County of Denver Official Ballot, John B. McGavran Scrapbooks Western History Collection WH445, Denver Public Library.

[4] 1928 abstract of election returns, Colorado Secretary of State.

This is to say that the "popular vote" is derived from the vote counts for presidential elector. Not the other way around.

The loss in democratic expression between the 1928 Colorado ballot and the 2016 ballot is significant. While Colorado's modern ballot access laws for nonmajor party candidates is particularly generous and likely one of the nation's best, the 2016 ballot offered Colorado voters twenty-two different ways (excluding write-ins) to cast their nine votes.

The 1928 ballot had six presidential tickets, but because voters could individually mix and match their six votes, this ballot featured 593,775 choices.[5]

That is to say, a voter had 593,775 different ways of casting their six votes.

Had the 2016 Colorado ballot shown the 198 candidates for presidential elector, and a voter could cast a mixed elector ballot, the ballot, instead of featuring 22 choices, would have featured 1.7x10^15 different ways for a voter to cast their 9 votes (that is, 1,071,781,612,741,840).

The difference between 1,071,781,612,741,840 and 22 is the democratic loss Colorado voters experienced in 2016.[6]

Here's another example.

---

[5] This is calculated with the combinations formula, where n is the number of candidates for Presidential Elector, and r is the amount of votes each voter has for Elector/the quantity of Electors the state has:

$$C(n, r) = \frac{n!}{r! \times (n - r)!}$$

C is the number of combinations

n is the total number of objects in the set

r is the number of choosing objects from the set

For simplicity, the combination calculations used in this book assume voters use all the votes available to them. A greater set of combinations exist when one adds combinations in which voters do not cast all their votes (Colorado 1928: 768,211 vs 593,775).

[6] 1,071,781,612,741,818.

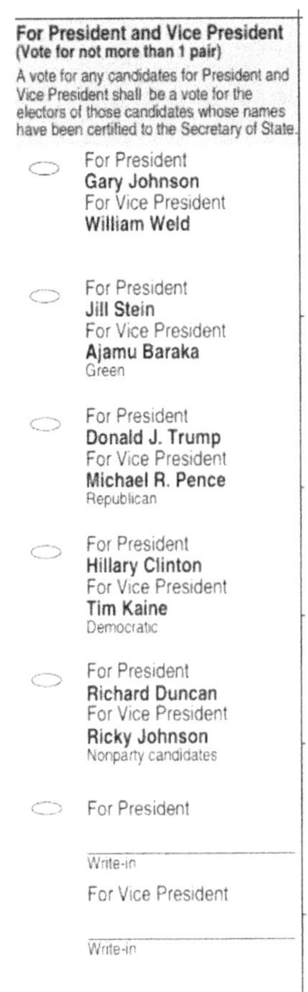

Figure 3.6 2016 Ohio Presidential ballot

This is the 2016 Ohio ballot:[7]

In 2016 Ohio voters had five ballot choices (without write-ins.) That means that these Ohio ballots had five ways for voters to cast their 18 votes.

This is the 1924 Ohio Presidential Elector ballot.[8] Like the 2016 Ohio

---

[7] Ohio's ballot rotation, which means every candidate has an equal chance to be at the top of the ticket (in other words, one out of every five Ohioans had a ballot like this one) is the national model, and is likely the best in the world.

[8] *Columbus Dispatch* (published as Columbus Evening Dispatch), October 29, 1924, Columbus, Ohio, Page 30.

ballot, it also features five presidential tickets. But in 1924 Ohio voters could mix and match their votes for presidential elector.

DEMOCRATIC TICKET	REPUBLICAN TICKET	INDEPENDENT PROGRESSIVE TICKET	COMMONWEALTH LAND TICKET	SOCIALIST LABOR TICKET
For President, JOHN W DAVIS	For President, CALVIN COOLIDGE	For President, ROBERT M. LAFOLLETTE	For President, W. J. WALLACE	For President, FRANK T. JOHNS
For Vice President, CHARLES W. BRYAN	For Vice President, CHARLES G. DAWES	For Vice President, BURTON K. WHEELER	For Vice President, J. C. LINCOLN	For Vice President, VERNE L. REYNOLDS
For Electors of President and Vice President, CLAUDE M. MEEKER	For Electors of President and Vice President, GEORGE H. CLARK	For Electors of President and Vice President, WARREN S. STONE	For Electors of President and Vice President, HARRY T. AMMON	For Electors of President and Vice President, FRANK HEIN
JUDSON HARMON	CHARLES W MONTGOMERY	MRS. JEWELL ZIEGLER	WILLIAM FEATHER	MICHAEL KATSARAS
ALFRED M COHEN	GEORGE PUCHTA	W. M. LEISERSON	HOWARD M. HOLMES	THOMAS MOODY
L N PRICE	FRED E. WESSELMANN	JERRY J. GALVIN	HENRY P. BOYNTON	SAMUEL WALD
WM. E. MURPHY	J. W. MYERS	H. R. KARNS	GORDON MACKLIN	GEORGE S. BARBEE
JOHN L. SULLIVAN	JAS. WARD KEYT	MRS. DELLA N. McCORMICK	J. C. McGREGOR	G. L. STEINBROOK
CHARLES W PALMER	DAVIS B. JOHNSON	C. A. BOLIN	J. J. CULBERTSON	W. T. WILLIAMS
SHERMAN S. JONES	A. T. HOLCOMB	MRS. DAISY C. MILLARD	FRANK HILLENKAMP	JOE BERRICK
WILLIAM T HAVILAND	NEWTON H. FAIRBANKS	MRS. EVELYN F. STIRES	ALBERT DAVIS	ERNEST PAZDERSKI
CARL WATSON	CLARENCE M. CESSNA	L. E. BARTH	EDMUND VANCE COOKE	GEORGE GRUMMITT
EMERY D. POTTER	MARY LOCKE HURIN	ALFRED HENDERSON	HARRY H. KLINE	PETER FABER
CHARLES J McCARTHY	JOHN FINSTERWALD	MRS. DORA BACHMAN	C. R. SWICKARD	JOHN HEIDENREICH
E C RUTTER	JOHN D. DAVIS	JERRY MINCHER	WILBUR B. LUTTON	SAM VOLCOFF
FRED J HEER	WALTER A. JONES	MRS. MAE NEWBURN	M. C. YEAGLE	FRANK KALCEC
WILLIAM HERNER	JOHN D. MACK	E. E. EISENBARTH	F. N. FLICK	WESELIN NUATEV
ERNEST H. CLINEDINST	V. W. FILLATRAULT	MRS. VIRGINIA D. GREEN	ARTHUR MORCOMB	
MRS. MAME WATSON	MILTON H. TURNER	HARRY DECHEND	W. A. CRONENBERGER	
C. H. LEY	WILLIAM T. KUHNS	GEORE W. BIDDLE	F. E. COTTIER	
E. M. DOUGLAS	THOMAS R. BARNES	S. B. MARVIN	HENRY GROTHE	
MRS. SARAH E FRAISER	EDW McKINLEY	MRS. NORMA W. JACKSON	HELENA M. MINICH	
LYNN B. GRIFFITH	J. D. WADDELL	LOUIS OROTSTEIN	GEORGE J. FOYER	
HUGH DUFFY	SAMUEL B. MICHELL	W. A. OULSINGER	HERMAN BIEDER	
GEO. W HOPKINS	A. J MITCHELL	ERNEST B. LANE	CYRIL J. BATH	
ARCHIE KENNEL	ELISABETH C. T. MILLER	GILBERT S. COX	JOHN S. PASKINS	

Figure 3.7 1924 Ohio Presidential Elector ballot

Back then, Ohio had twenty-three electoral votes. This ballot features 106 candidates, with 1.12×10^{23} different ways for a voter to cast their twenty-three votes (112,380,720,985,107,824, 012,400).

Note at the top of this ballot are the *straight-ticket devices*.

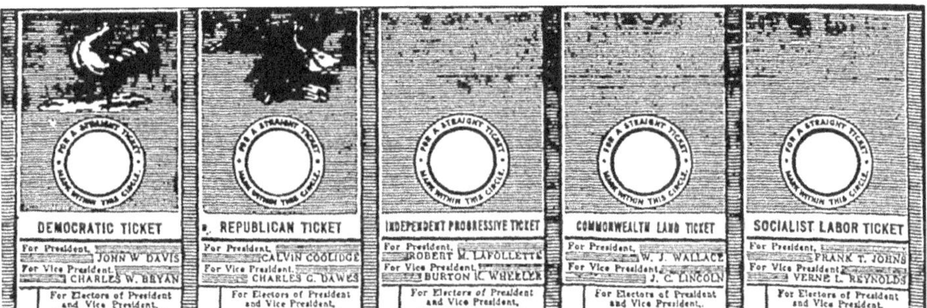

Figure 3.8 1924 Ohio Presidential Elector ballot close-up on straight ticket devices

While voters did have all those choices, they could also simply mark the circle at the top of the page and cast all twenty-three of their votes for one slate of presidential elector candidates.

Beginning in the early twentieth century, and accelerating rapidly in the 1930s and 1940s,[9] state legislatures began to remove the names of the candidates for presidential elector, and with it, the ability of voters to mix and match their votes.[10] What they left on the ballot were the straight-ticket devices, which they relabeled with the names of the presidential nominees those candidates for presidential elector were pledged to.

---

[9] A table of when states switched is in the Appendix A.

[10] In 2020 Arizona, Idaho, Louisiana, North Dakota, and South Dakota still have the names of the candidates for presidential elector on the ballot, but like the rest of the states, removed the individual selection mechanisms and left only the straight ticket devices.

which became this

Vote for all eighteen Libertarian Party Electors
Vote for all eighteen Green Party Electors
Vote for all eighteen Republican Electors
Vote for all eighteen Democratic Electors
Vote for all eighteen nonparty Duncan/Johnson Electors

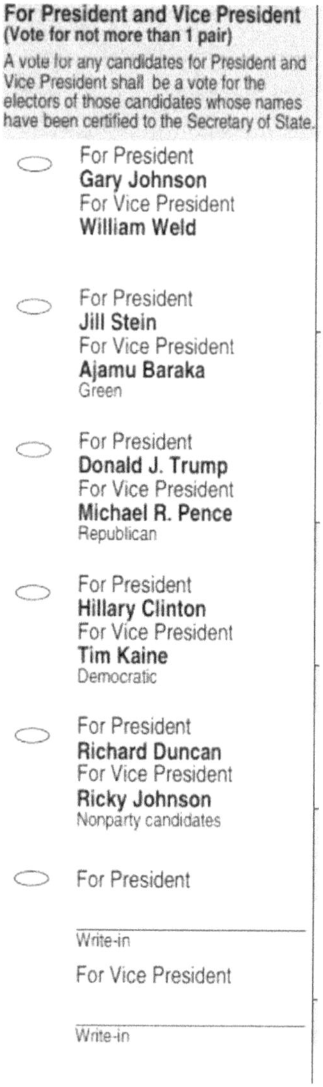

For President and Vice President
(Vote for not more than 1 pair)

A vote for any candidates for President and Vice President shall be a vote for the electors of those candidates whose names have been certified to the Secretary of State.

For President
Gary Johnson
For Vice President
William Weld

For President
Jill Stein
For Vice President
Ajamu Baraka
Green

For President
Donald J. Trump
For Vice President
Michael R. Pence
Republican

For President
Hillary Clinton
For Vice President
Tim Kaine
Democratic

For President
Richard Duncan
For Vice President
Ricky Johnson
Nonparty candidates

For President

Write-in

For Vice President

Write-in

Figure 3.9 The evolution of the Presidential Elector Straight Ticket Device into the modern Mandatory Straight Ticket

This book calls the modern ballot the "mandatory straight ticket."[11]

What is remarkable about the mandatory straight ticket is that it gives voters the illusion of control while simultaneously denying it to them.

It is a classic bait and switch: The bait is the illusion of control granted by "directly" voting for the president and the switch is the voting combinations lost through the mandatory straight ticket.

---

[11] Perhaps more accurately it's the presidential elector mandatory straight ticket. It is normally called the "presidential short-ballot," which is a misleading euphemism. (The presidential elector straight ticket should not be confused with the full-ballot straight ticket that some states have, which allows a voter to vote one party for all offices on the ballot. For an example of a ballot with both a full-ballot straight ticket device and a presidential elector straight ticket device, see the 1908 Nebraska ballot in Appendix C.)

When "Winner-Takes-All" States Weren't

WHILE IT IS TRUE THAT in most of American history voters did not mix and match their Electors (why they didn't is discussed later) they did enough to cause at least thirteen times in US history where a state had a mixed presidential elector result:[12]

---

[12] Svend Petersen, *A Statistical History of the American Presidential Elections* (New York: Ungar, 1963) https://babel.hathitrust.org/cgi/pt?id=mdp.39015041854988;view=1up; seq=7.

This list only shows when a statewide election for electors had a mixed result due to voters splitting their tickets. Mixed results also happen when a state has presidential elector districts, and each voter has one vote for presidential elector in their district. Examples of this include New York State 1824 and 1828, Michigan 1892, and today in Maine and Nebraska (kind of: not all of those states' electors are elected.)

Year and State	Number of Statewide Electors	Democratic Electors Elected	Republican Electors Elected	Populist Electors Elected	Notes
1860 New Jersey	7	3	4		Splinter groups printed fusion ballots
1880 California	6	5	1		
1892 California	9	8	1		
1892 North Dakota	3		1	2	State Democratic party supported a fusion Democratic-Populist ticket. One of the Populist electors voted for the Democratic Ticket
1892 Ohio	23	1	22		
1892 Oregon	4	3		1	
1896 California	9	1	8		
1896 Kentucky	13	1	12		
1904 Maryland	8	7	1		
1908 Maryland	8	6	2		
1912 California	13	2	11		
1916 West Virginia	8	1	7		
1960 Alabama	11	5 pledged 6 unpledged			A Presidential Elector primary created a list of 11 Democratic elector candidates with the 5 pledged/6 unpledged split. Therefore this split did not occur in the General Election, but in the Primary Election.

Figure 4.1 Historic Mixed Statewide Presidential Elector results

CHAPTER 5

Early American Ballots

MOST VOTERS IN THE TWENTIETH century received presidential elector ballots with the mandatory straight ticket.

From roughly 1880 to 1930, most voters received presidential elector ballots with the ability to mix and match their votes.

Prior to 1880, state election officials did not give ballots to the voters. Instead, voters received the ballot from the political parties who handed them out. On polling day, the voter dropped their preferred ballot into the ballot box.

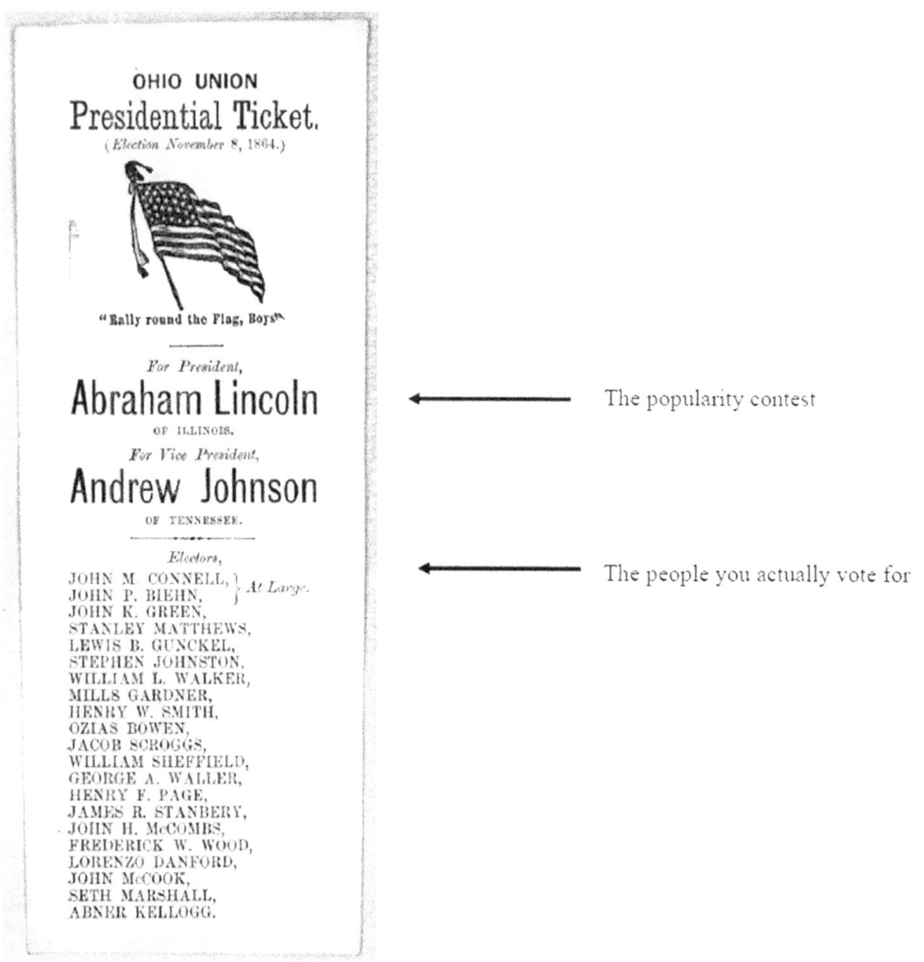

Figure 5.1 1864 Ohio Republican Presidential Ticket[13]

At the top was the party's popularity contest. That is what the party wanted voters to focus on in order to get them to vote for the party's candidates for presidential elector, which are found at the bottom of the ballot.

---

[13] Ohio Union Presidential Ticket. Presidential Ticket, Election November 8, 1864; For President, Abraham Lincoln of Illinois, For Vice President Andrew Johnson of Tennessee. Columbus, 1864. Retrieved from Library of Congress: https://www. loc.gov/item/ rbpe.1370220c/

This ballot was called the "presidential ticket" and it's where we get the name for this concept.

Mixing and matching electors was possible at this time period, as shown by the election results in 1860 New Jersey. That particular result occurred through splinter groups printing off a mixed ballot. It could also occur through a voter editing a presidential ticket (crossing out candidates they didn't want to vote for and writing in candidates they did) or *handwriting in their own ballot.* We will come back to this method.

Why "Winner-Takes-All"

AMERICANS ARE CONFUSED ABOUT THE concept of winner-takes-all. No state has the concept of winner-takes-all in their elections laws because it doesn't really exist. There is no such thing as a "popular vote" that is then manipulated into a state's Electoral College result. Nor is there any property of the Electoral College that demands winner-takes-all. Voters vote for electors directly, and it is a side effect of the ballot design that creates the winner-takes-all effect.

But that side effect is not accidental. There is a beneficiary of the winner-takes-all system, it's just not the voters or democracy.

Nor is it the states. There is no benefit to California or Texas (or Californians/Texans) to have a binary winner-takes-all result.

As an Ohio voter, the novelty of being at the center of the American political discussion is fleeting. I can't determine any long-term benefit the state has accrued from being a swing state.

The beneficiaries of winner-takes-all are the two major political parties. It is they who removed the full gamut of democratic choice offered by the mixed elector ballots, forcing voters to cast all their votes for electors one way or another.

It should be said that there were other factors as well. The mandatory straight ticket emerged with the lever-based voting machines of the early twentieth century. These machines were difficult to configure for long ballots, particularly when it's multiple votes for one office. This wasn't a problem with paper ballots, but undoubtedly the difficulty of the mixed elector ballot on the lever machines played a role in the adoption of the mandatory straight ticket. (A curious situation where it's the technology that dictated the democratic process.)

The early twentieth century also had a "short ballot movement" whose adherents (including Woodrow Wilson) believed that the voting process was too difficult and complex for voters: voters had too many choices and they were making bad decisions because of it.[14] The solution was to eliminate some elected offices. Largely speaking this did not happen, but it was the mandatory straight ticket (under the euphemism "presidential short ballot") that ended up becoming a national standard.

At the same time that states were switching to the mandatory straight tickets, they also were dramatically increasing the difficulty for parties other than the Republicans and Democrats to get onto the ballot. It is only recently that ballot access for minor parties and independent candidates has become a little easier.[15] In much of the time period from the 1930s to the 1990s, many Americans only had two parties on their ballots.

I was particularly struck by this editorial in the *Jefferson City Post-Tribune* in Missouri from 1933. This article was discussing the Missouri state legislature's decision to switch to the mandatory straight ticket and says

One of the good measures now pending in the General Assembly is that sponsored by Senator Rollins of Columbia for the shortening of the ballot. Instead of the fifteen presidential electors Mr. Rollins proposes that only the names of the candidates for president and vice-president be printed on the ballot. That is not only simpler but it is much more sensible and will be much better understood by the

---

[14] Curiously, early proponents of the short ballot movement included the League of Women Voters, whose advocacy for simplified ballots coincided with their advocacy for women's voting rights.

[15] For an understanding of the enormous amount of litigation and current events on ballot access across the US, see Richard Winger's Ballot Access News at ballot-access.org.

voter, and will be heartily sanctioned by them. This measure should receive serious and favorable consideration.

The legislature might well go a little further and provide the short ballot for the state ticket. That will greatly simplify the voting process and it will to the government that simplicity responsibility it has long needed. The present Legislature is making an attempt to give more control and power to the Governor. The short ballot will do this in a simple way.[16]

In effect, they saw no need for voters to be presented with anything else other than two choices on the ballot, red or blue. The ultimate in winner-takes-all ballots, where all the candidates for public office are hidden from voters, not just the presidential electors.

Certainly that would be the ideal for the main political parties.

The Democratic and Republican parties have a codependent relationship with each other: one party cannot call it a democracy without the other party. Over the course of American history, they have both engaged in various electoral shenanigans, such as gerrymandering or making it near impossible for minor parties to get on state ballots[17], but they never went so far as to try to remove the other party from the ballot.

---

[16] "A good measure," *Jefferson City Post-Tribune,* Jefferson City, Missouri, March 7, 1933, Page 4.

[17] Major parties often use legal processes to get minor parties off the ballot, typically by pointing out to elections officials/courts paperwork errors.
In 2020 the Democratic Party initiated legal action in an attempt to remove from the ballot Green Party candidates/the full Green Party ticket in Montana, Wisconsin, Pennsylvania and Texas.
In 2020 the Republican Party initiated legal action in an attempt to remove from the ballot Libertarian Party candidates/the full Libertarian Party ticket in Oregon, Illinois and Texas.
The major parties do not attempt to remove each other from the ballot. I've seen enough elections paperwork to say that their candidacy petitions are not error free and the opportunity is there. (See the footnote in Appendix B.)
(Information from ballot-access.org. This footnote is a gross simplification of this activity this year.)

Without the other party, it's not a democracy and they can't legitimatize their power.

However, the two parties still wanted to control as much as possible. Their preference was two parties on the ballot, and they often made decisions that contribute to a winner-takes-all effect.

The flip side of winner-takes-all is loser-gets-nothing. For the two political parties, loser-gets-nothing is an acceptable risk for the opportunity to take all the power *on their terms.*

There is another advantage to the mandatory straight ticket (and the popularity contest that accompanies it) in that it encourages voters to vote the popularity contest down-ticket to other offices. Voters seize on the popularity contest, choose one Presidential ticket over another, and carry that preference down to the other offices on the ballot. In this way, you could say that the popularity contest has its own secondary winner-takes-all effect.

This effect is diminished when voters think of their multiple votes for electors as being a gradient they can use to express a political preference with more subtlety and complexity than merely the single popular vote for President.

In other words, when a voter chooses to split their votes for electors between different parties, that voter will be more likely to see all the offices on the ballot as similarly splittable. It is much harder for down-ticket politicians to ride on the coattails of the presidential nominee if voters are focusing their attention on the wide variety of elector combinations available.

Even when voters were presented with the names of the candidates for presidential elector, they were not encouraged to have a relationship with the candidates for presidential elector or the electors themselves.

The height of this is to hide the names of people the voters are voting for.

The electors were chosen by the parties to follow the instructions of the party, even when it makes no sense (more on that in a bit.) They have been subsequently bound by law (in many states) to follow the parties instructions, even when it is a pointless act.

The more relationship voters would have with the candidates or the electors, the less power the parties would have in the process of choosing the president. The political parties wanted party functionaries, not fully elected representatives.

Americans have long assumed that the elections system took the Electoral College and somehow manipulated it into a more democratic system through the popular vote. But that is backward; the popular vote has subordinated the Electoral College to the political parties. The mandatory straight ticket is evidence of that. Voters aren't allowed to experience the Electoral College as the full democratic institution that it could be.

With ballots that allow for mixing and matching of votes for electors and autonomous, unbound electors, voters would have the ability to reject the nominated candidates for the major parties. That's what the parties do not want, hence mandatory straight tickets and bound electors.

Whether a presidential elector is "faithless" to the voters or not is contextual. But the words for an elector who does something different than what their political parties nominated them to do, such as "disobedient," "faithless," or "gone rogue," are a reflection of what the political party thinks of them, and their relationship to the elector, not the voter and the voter's relationship to the elector.

"Winner-takes-all" and "loser-gets-nothing" might make sense for the political parties but makes no sense for voters or democracy.[18]

---

[18] Consider the scenario of 135 Democratic electors and 135 Republican electors equally choosing a President.

The problem for the two parties in this instance is that if the President messes up, one party can't blame the other for it.

Nor if the President does a good job, can one party or the other take full credit.

So winner-takes-all and loser-gets-nothing suits their purposes: "If we don't get all the power, let the other side have it fully and we can blame them."

Winner-takes-all feeds into the polarization of American politics. A president chosen equally by the two major parties is an unpolarized muddle which is less useful to the parties in their political campaigns.

The American people do not vote for the president. The power and influence of American voters would be maximized by fully investing ourselves in the elections contest that we participate in—the election of the electors. What happens now is our collective power is drained and minimized by a popularity contest that we have little control over. After all, the 2016 election results show that the American people do not participate in the popularity contest.

CHAPTER 7

Elector Bindings: When Voters Go Unrepresented in the Electoral College

In November 2016, 66 million Americans elected 232 Democratic presidential electors and 63 million Americans elected 306 Republican presidential electors.

As a thought experiment, let's say that on the day the Electoral College met (in Stage Two) these electors did exactly as they pledged, voting 232 for Clinton and 306 for Trump.

The result of that would have been the election of Donald Trump as president.

Even with two autonomous, defecting electors from the Republican 306 (which is what happened in 2016) the remaining 304 electors (with 270 needed for the win) made Trump the president.

What would have happened if all 232 Democratic presidential electors just stayed home and did nothing?

Well perhaps there might have been a couple less or a couple more defecting electors in the Republican 306, but most likely Trump would have had the 270 to become president.

So in effect, the 232 Democratic electors staying home and doing nothing would have led to the same result as all of them voting for Hillary Clinton.

Why is that? Remember, the political parties nominate party loyalists to be candidates for presidential elector. There was no one in the 306 Republican electors who would have been willing to vote Clinton. With no viable strategy for electing Clinton, voting for Clinton is equivalent to not doing anything at all. The Democratic electors could have stayed home with the same result.

In effect, the binding laws mean that voters for the electors representing the losing presidential ticket go *unrepresented* in Stage Two. (The flip side of winner-takes-all is loser-gets-nothing.)

The several states' binding laws work in different ways. In 2016 Washington state fined disobedient electors $1,000, Colorado removed an autonomous elector from office and replaced him with another[19], and in New Mexico being a disobedient elector is a felony with potential jail time.[20]

Why is it so desperately critical for the 232 Democratic electors to be "faithful" if doing so is the equivalent of not doing anything at all?

One problem is that there are no secondary mandates for the candidates for presidential elector. All they have is a primary mandate, which is vote for their parties' presidential tickets. There is no secondary mandate when that doesn't work out, and in 2016 the so-called "disobedient" or "faithless" electors attempted to work one out with themselves.

We could have candidates for presidential electors with secondary mandates (secondary choices they would make depending on circumstances). But to do so, the voters and the candidates have to have a relationship with each other, which they currently do not have, and the two main political parties are not interested to see develop. For the electors to have secondary mandates would mean the electors would have to have autonomy to negotiate among themselves.

This is what we are losing out on: what any one presidential elector is

---

[19] *Chiafalo v. Washington,* 591 U.S.___2020

[20] "Faithless Elector State Laws," FairVote, July 7, 2020, https://www.fairvote.org/faithless_elector_state_laws.

capable of doing is a function of the other 537. We don't know what's possible in Stage Two until after the election for electors (Stage One) is completed. Yet electors are bound to the Stage One candidates pointlessly.

The irony of this is that the Washington and Colorado electors who tried a plan B, namely a variety of different votes to prevent the election of Donald Trump, were acting in a way that was perfectly rational for the voters who elected them. Those electors were actually involved in Stage Two and represented/attempted to represent the voters who elected them.

The rest of them could have just stayed home.[21] Nevertheless, the states of Washington and Colorado (supported by almost all the others) went to the Supreme Court to ensure that voters in those states go unrepresented in Stage Two in the future. In doing so, those states were not defending the interests of their voters.

In insisting that the electors vote for a nonviable candidate, the states were defending loser-gets-nothing so that winner-takes-all could survive. Here it created the bizarre circumstance under which the states insisted that Democratic electors help elect Donald Trump[22] by voting for a nonviable candidate, instead of working with other electors to create a different outcome. This weird situation exists because it works for the parties, not the people.

Why can't American voters have a relationship with the people they

---

[21] If the Electoral College deadlocks and no one gets 270 votes, Congress will choose among the pool of individuals the electors voted for. That is a potential strategy for the electors but it only requires one elector to vote for that individual.

[22] Had this situation been reversed and instead 306 Democratic and 232 Republican electors had been elected, the argument here indeed is that the 232 Republican electors could have pressed the 306 Democratic electors for an alternative to Clinton. That could have resulted in a less-polarizing presidential selection, but it is by all means a possibility worth having because its existence means the 232 Democratic and 306 Republican electors of 2016 would have had the opportunity to select a less-polarizing presidential selection than the one selected in 2016. By eliminating the elector bindings, and leaving the winner-takes-all philosophy behind them, we can come to less-polarizing electoral results.

elect?[23] The current system makes voters prisoners of the popularity contest. If voters had a relationship with the presidential electors, then we could broaden this system into one that is less polarized, more flexible, and more democratic.

---

[23] What's notable is that voters in 2016 did have a relationship with the electors—admittedly, after the election, but voters contacting electors to ask them to vote for or against a particular presidential nominee was a wonderful development—it was the voters treating the presidential electors as the democratic representatives they are, and not merely as bureaucratic, anonymous party functionaries.

CHAPTER 8

Elections in East Germany

THE GERMAN DEMOCRATIC REPUBLIC (1949 to 1990, a.k.a., East Germany) did not have free and fair elections.[24]

When a voter received a ballot, it was for a list of people predetermined by the East German Communist party. A voter could strike out a name (but not add another), however there was no way of doing that privately. A voter was expected to fold the ballot immediately and deposit it in the ballot box—and they were observed to ensure they did exactly this. (In East German slang "to go folding" ("falten gehen") meant to go voting.)

---

[24] With the exception of the last one in 1990. Featured is a local election ballot for East Berlin from May 7, 1989.

Stimmzettel (ballot paper for election to the Stadtbezirksversammlung (assembly of deputies,) district Lichtenberg, East Berlin, German Democratic Republic, May 7, 1989,) "More Than Just an Oxymoron? Democracy in the German Democratic Republic," April 10, 2016, https://historyned.blog/2016/04/10/more-than-just-an-oxymoron-democracy-in-the-german-democratic-republic/.

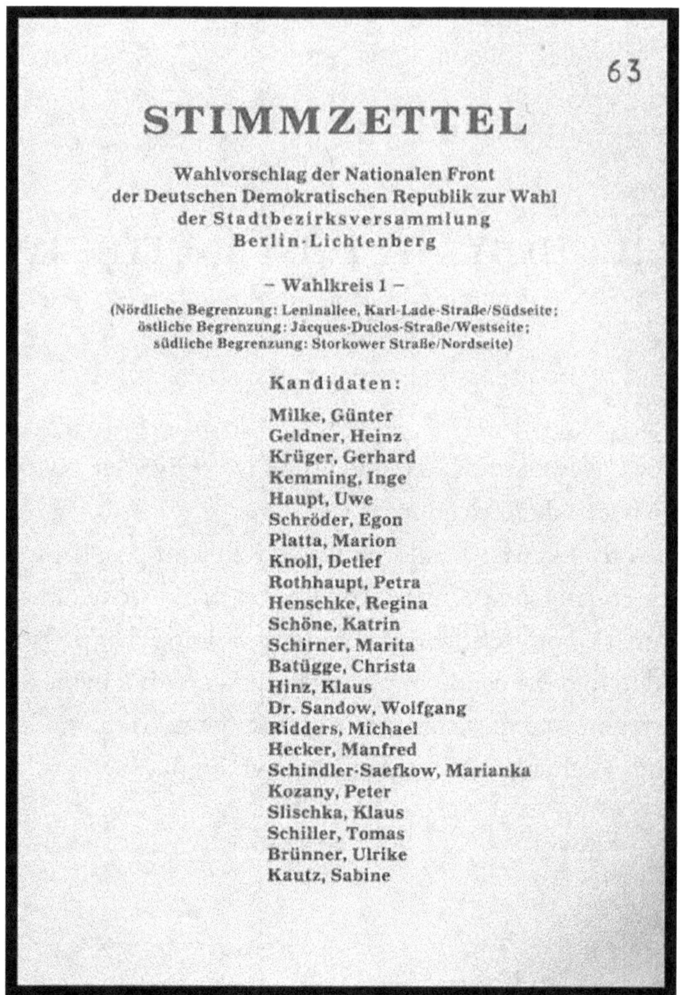

Figure 8.1 Ballot Paper for local election, East Berlin, German Democratic Republic, May 1989. This ballot contains no instructions for the voter.

Elections (and life) in the United States are very different from East Germany.

The two were not normally compared.

But the mandatory straight tickets used to vote for presidential electors have a lot in common with the former East German one-party ballots.

The main difference is that East German voters received one ballot with prefilled choices which they couldn't change … and American voters in the twentieth century received two presidential elector ballots with prefilled choices they couldn't change.

It is sobering to compare the last century of American democracy to that of the East German state. (America was still a democracy, after all; there was at least one other ballot available even if it were fixed.)

But I find the comparison enlightening and a key to understanding American democracy and how the mandatory straight tickets have influenced US history.

—m—

It is curious to note that in the recent Supreme Court decision on presidential elector autonomy (*Chiafalo v. Washington*), a key section rejecting that autonomy says:

The Electors argue that three simple words stand in for more explicit language about discretion. Article II, §1 first names the members of the Electoral College: "electors." The Twelfth Amendment then says that electors shall "vote" and that they shall do so by "ballot." The "plain meaning" of those terms, the Electors say, requires electors to have "freedom of choice." If the States could control their votes, "the electors would not be 'Electors,' and their 'vote by Ballot' would not be a 'vote.'"

But those words need not always connote independent choice. Suppose a person always votes in the way his spouse, pastor, or union tells them to. We might question the person's judgment, but we would have no problem saying that he or she "votes" or fills in a "ballot." In those cases, the choice is in someone else's hands, but the words still apply because they can signify a mechanical act. Or similarly, suppose in a system allowing proxy voting (a common practice in the founding era), the proxy acts on clear instructions from the principal, with no freedom of choice. Still, we might well say that he cast a "ballot" or "voted," though the preference registered was not his own. For that matter, some elections give the voter no real choice because there is only one name on a ballot (consider an old Soviet election, or even a down-ballot race in this country). Yet if the person in the voting booth goes through the motions, we consider him or her to have voted. The point of all these examples is to show that although voting and discretion are usually combined, voting is still voting when discretion departs. Maybe most telling, switch from hypotheticals to the members of the electoral college. For centuries now, as we'll later show, almost all have considered themselves bound to vote for their party's (and the state voters') preference. Yet there is no better description for what they do in the Electoral College than "vote" by "ballot." And all these years later, everyone still calls them "electors"—and not wrongly, because even though they vote without discretion, they do indeed elect a president.

In effect, the Supreme Court says that "voting" can be something with discretion or it could be without, and specifically offered the example of a Soviet elections ballot. In short, the Supreme Court compared presidential electors without autonomy to a Soviet election, and this book compares the process of voting for those electors on mandatory straight tickets as similar to a Communist block election.

In other words, both Stage One and Two share Soviet characteristics.

The East German use of the term "to go folding" reflected the fact that voters knew they were not participating in a democratic event, but in a theatrical one. (Theater that if a citizen didn't participate in, or deviated from their role, might be punished by the State.)

American elections are much freer, and even at their worst, offer no less than two choices.

But the popularity contest is theatrical. Americans are shown a film about two people in the popularity contest, and at the end of it are given a red ballot or a blue one, one of which they can drop in the box.

But they aren't told what the ballots do, and the people they are actually voting for do not appear in the film.

Often there is an alignment between the theatrical vote and the real one such that the winner of the popularity contest becomes the president.

When this occurs, it can give a veneer of democratic legitimacy to the theatrical event.

It doesn't always occur.

Voters Stuck in a Theater: Why Voters Didn't Mix and Match Ballots When They Could?

I BEGIN THIS EXPLANATION BY showing these two sample ballots found in an 1896 West Virginia newspaper[25] and an 1892 Ohio newspaper.[26]

---

[25] Sample ballot, *The Wheeling daily intelligencer.* (Wheeling, W. Va.), October 27, 1896. Chronicling America: Historic American Newspapers, Library of Congress, https:// chroniclingamerica.loc.gov/lccn/sn84026844/1896-10-27/ed-1/seq-6/.

[26] Sample ballot, *The Ohio Democrat* (Logan, Ohio), November 5 1892. Chronicling America: Historic American Newspapers, Library of Congress, https://chroniclingamerica.loc.gov/ lccn/sn87075048/1892-11-05/ed-1/seq-1/

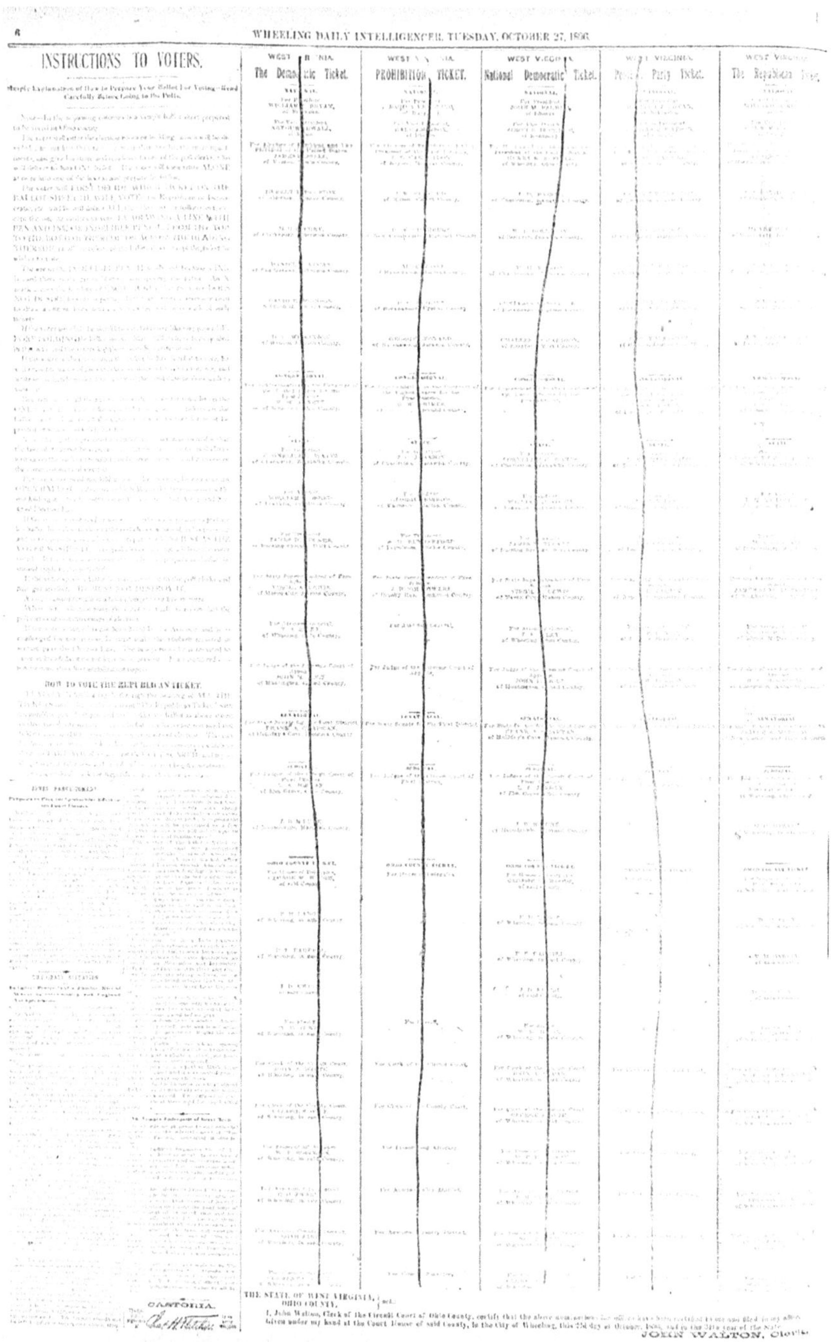
8 WHEELING DAILY INTELLIGENCER, TUESDAY, OCTOBER 27, 1896.

INSTRUCTIONS TO VOTERS.

HOW TO VOTE THE REPUBLICAN TICKET.

PROHIBITION TICKET.

National Democratic Ticket.

CASTORIA.

THE STATE OF WEST VIRGINIA,
OHIO COUNTY,

JOHN WALTON, Clerk.

Figure 9.1 1896 West Virginia Sample Ballot

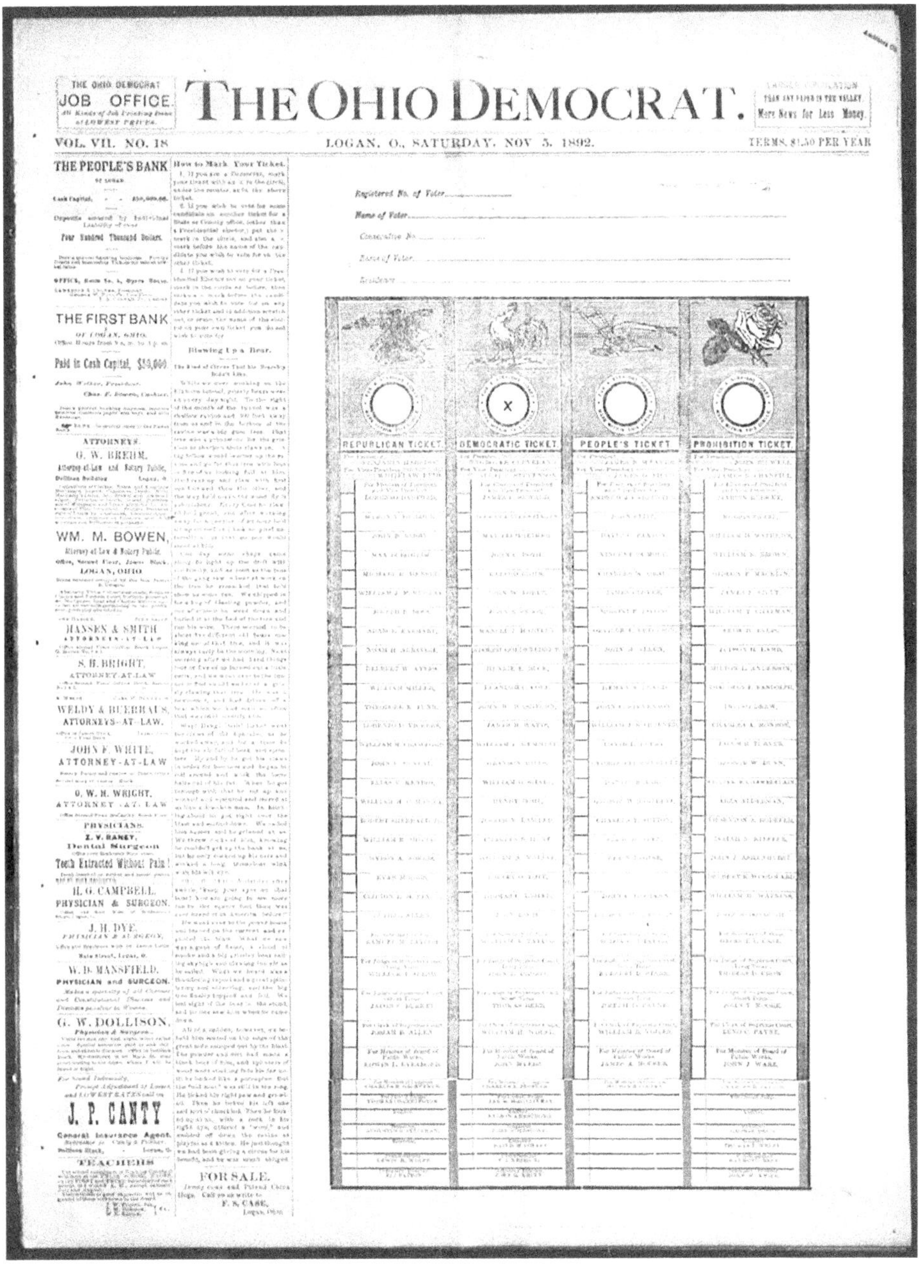

THE OHIO DEMOCRAT JOB OFFICE

THE OHIO DEMOCRAT.

More News for Less Money.

VOL. VII. NO. 18 LOGAN, O., SATURDAY, NOV 5, 1892. TERMS, $1.50 PER YEAR

THE PEOPLE'S BANK

THE FIRST BANK

Paid in Cash Capital, $50,000

ATTORNEYS.

G. W. BREHM,

WM. M. BOWEN,

LOGAN, OHIO

HANSEN & SMITH

S. H. BRIGHT, ATTORNEY-AT-LAW

WELDY & HUEBRAUS, ATTORNEYS-AT-LAW.

JOHN F. WHITE, ATTORNEY-AT-LAW

O. W. H. WRIGHT, ATTORNEY-AT-LAW

PHYSICIANS.

Dental Surgeon

Teeth Extracted Without Pain!

H. G. CAMPBELL, PHYSICIAN & SURGEON.

J. H. DYE

W. D. MANSFIELD.

G. W. DOLLISON,

J. P. CANTY

TEACHERS

How to Mark Your Ticket.

Blowing Up a Bear.

FOR SALE.

REPUBLICAN TICKET. DEMOCRATIC TICKET. PEOPLE'S TICKET. PROHIBITION TICKET.

Figure 9.2 1892 Ohio Sample Ballot

Polarization of the nation's media is not a new thing. In American history quite a lot of Americans lived in communities with two newspapers, one Republican leaning, the other Democratic leaning. In the first image the *Wheeling Daily Intelligencer* is showing readers a sample West Virginia ballot that is marked for the Republican straight ticket. (At that time in West Virginia voters crossed out the candidates/tickets they didn't want.[27])

In the second image, the *Ohio Democrat* shows its partisan colors (if the name didn't give it away) by showing voters how to vote the straight Democratic ticket (on this ballot that would have been all offices, not just presidential elector).[28]

Faced with a media that didn't explore the idea of casting mixed ballots, and political parties who definitely didn't want to see it happen, it was not in the public discourse.

The only "election" voters were aware of was the popularity contest. Voters naturally wanted to be involved in the contest presented to them, even if it weren't the one they actually were voting in. That's the reality show the voters had at hand, and to vote in a way not shown on that reality show might feel less satisfying, like it's a "wasted vote."

Ultimately voters didn't really understand how this process worked. After all, I'd like to believe if they did back then, then we would today. Instead we have this strange notion of the popularity vote determining but being filtered through the Electoral College.[29]

---

[27] According to the instructions, a voter wanting to cast a mixed ballot in this election needed to choose one ticket, cross out the rest, cross out the candidates on the remaining ticket they didn't want and then transpose the names of the candidates they did want from the other tickets and write them in next to the stricken-out candidates they were replacing. Quite a complex operation for a voter to do in the five minutes the voter had in the poll booth under law.

[28] As an aside, I did locate newspapers giving instructions to voters on how to vote for other parties, such as the Progressive and Socialist. If I find them again, they'll appear in the next book.

[29] This is in spite of the fact that there were ballots with no straight ticket devices, such as the 1928 Colorado in Chapter 3, or the 1892 California in Appendix C, in which voters would have known they were casting multiple votes for Presidential Elector.

CHAPTER 10

Leaving the Theater: Working around the Mandatory Straight Ticket with the Mixed Elector Ballot

THIS BOOK HAS CALLED IT the mandatory straight ticket.

The argument for this terminology is because with voters not knowing that they are casting multiple votes simultaneously on a straight ticket, and even in the one state with a known legal mechanism for casting a mixed elector ballot (Pennsylvania), voters are not told this.

This book believes, however, that the straight-ticket device on the forty-nine affected state ballots can't *truly* be mandatory because it would imply that voters *must* use the straight-ticket device. That would be a disturbing and profoundly undemocratic outcome, which would make our elections share quite a lot with the East German elections.

Besides, the literature on the "presidential short ballot" said that it was never intended to preclude a voter from mixing and matching their votes:

Since the ballot contained a blank column or blank lines for the write-in privilege, this group arrangement did not infringe upon the right of the voter who wished to choose his electoral candidate from more than one party.[30]

Since the modern ballot only has a straight-ticket device, the proposed solution around this is to submit a personally written or typed ballot with the names of your votes for presidential elector.

There is a history in American elections of voters submitting their own ballots. As mentioned before, it was the only way a voter could vote a non-party ballot in the elections prior to the introduction of the state printed ballot.

Even in the times of state printed ballots, submitting a handwritten/typed ballot is a necessary option if a state runs out of ballots or there is an inability to get a voter a ballot in a timely manner.

The method used for counting is that the election's authority figures out the intent of the voter and records a vote for that candidate(s). This would be done all over America at the county level by the local board of elections, which are nonpartisan.[31]

Generally in modern times candidates for elections have to be preregistered as a candidate with elections officials in order for a vote to be counted.

That applies to both categories of candidates:

- Independent and party candidates who are listed on the ballot (remember, in a strict technical sense, it is the presidential electors who are on the ballot, not the Presidential nominees).
- Presidential ticket nominees who are on a "write-in" ballot. These are

---

[30] Albright, Spencer D. "The Presidential Short Ballot." *The American Political Science Review*, vol. 34, no. 5, 1940, pp. 955–959. *JSTOR*, www.jstor.org/stable/1949218. Accessed 11 Aug. 2020.

[31] Your county board of elections is staffed by your fellow Americans who have been through the difficulties in 2020 as much as you have. They want a good and trusted election as much as anyone else, and they can only work with state law, not against it. Please treat them with courtesy as they do their jobs, and as a reminder, America will need plenty of poll workers this year. If you can take the health risk, please volunteer.

candidates who are preregistered and a voter can vote for them, but they do not appear on the ballot.

This means that there is, at least in modern times, the inability to cast a vote for a person who has not registered themselves as a candidate. That vote will typically go uncounted.

But the two preregistered categories above are rich in candidates for presidential elector. Voters in the forty-nine states can obtain their state's list of *Candidates for Presidential Elector* in October.

From that list, a voter can choose their candidates for presidential elector and put them down on a ballot that, at least for a Colorado voter in 2020, might look like this:

Presidential Elector Ballot
November 3, 2020 election
City and County of Denver, Colorado

I would like to cast my 9 votes for the following electors:

From the Citrus party list:

Calabrian Clementine
Hardy Mandarin

From the Pear party list:

Pink Bartlett
Fresh Starkrimson

From the Apple party list:

Golden Delicious
Newton Wonder

From the independent (Cherokee Purple Tomato for President/Haas Avocado for Vice-President) list:

Bitter Melon
Green Cauliflower
Canary Melon

Instructions to Board of Elections: Listed above are votes for registered candidates for Presidential Elector with the Colorado Secretary of State. Record each vote directly in the abstract.

Figure 10.1 Hypothetical Sample Mixed Elector Ballot for 2020 Election (Colorado)

Send that document in with your absentee ballot.

Will this work?

It certainly will in Pennsylvania, as Pennsylvania has the right under law for voters to do this.[32] (Hypothetically the state printed ballots should have the room for a Pennsylvanian to write in their twenty votes. The author has asked the Pennsylvania Secretary of State to confirm this, but has received no response at the time of finalizing this book.)

The author, an Ohioan, believes it will work in Ohio, based on conversations with state and county electoral authorities. Ohio's constitution prohibits straight tickets generally, but voters "may" use it for presidential elector.[33]

I personally will be writing in "see attached" in the write-in field. That seems reasonable.

It should work in Colorado, as Colorado's constitution says it is a right for voters to vote directly for presidential electors.[34] (Colorado's Secretary of State has not responded to the question of whether they will count a mixed elector ballot.)

For all the other states, I wrote elections officials and asked them directly if they would count a mixed elector ballot submitted by a voter.

As of the date this book was finalized, the following states have said that voters must use the mandatory straight ticket on the state printed ballot based on the

---

[32] Pennsylvania statute 25 Pa. Stat. § 2963: "To vote for individual candidates for presidential elector, write or stamp their names in the blank spaces provided for that purpose under the title 'Presidential Electors.' … There shall be left at the end of the group of candidates for President and Vice-President of the United States under the title 'Presidential Electors,' as many blank spaces as there are presidential electors to be elected, in which spaces the elector may insert, by writing or stamping, the names of any individual candidates for presidential electors for whom he desires to vote."

[33] Ohio Constitution, Article V, Section 2a: "An elector may vote for candidates (other than candidates for electors of President and Vice-President of the United States and other than candidates for governor and lieutenant governor) only and in no other way than by indicating his vote for each candidate separately from the indication of his vote for any other candidate." Note that a different section of the state constitution requires the straight ticket device for Governor and Lt. Governor. This section of the state constitution comes after a 1936 state Supreme Court case that rejected a political party's plea for mixed elector ballots.

[34] Colorado Constitution, Schedule 20 of the Constitutional Convention of 1876: "The general assembly shall provide that after the year eighteen hundred and seventy-six the electors of the electoral college shall be chosen by direct vote of the people."

idea that state law did not have a legal mechanism to count a mixed elector ballot and/or the state had no law for dealing with a nonstandard ballot:

Alabama	Alaska	Indiana[35]	Montana	New Hampshire
New Mexico	Oklahoma	Rhode Island	Utah	Virginia

Figure 10.2 States with election officials responding to author indicating that in 2020 a mixed elector ballot would not be counted

None of the states above responded saying that there was a legal requirement to vote only the straight ticket, just that they had no mechanism for dealing with a mixed elector ballot. Nor have states challenged the key issue—that voters are casting multiple votes simultaneously which they are unable to separate due to the mandatory straight ticket.[36]

As of the date this book was finalized, the following states have not responded to the question:

---

[35] A special note about Indiana: Indiana has dealt with this problem before, as noted in an article in *The Indianapolis Star* on Wednesday, Oct 29, 1924, Page 1: "Pasters to Permit Splitting Elector Votes on Machines: State and County Boards decide on use of gummed stripes next Tuesday despite approval of previous plan in order to meet objections of those who raised issue that law would be violated unless casting of mixed ballot was made possible."

[36] Ultimately, none of the states have disconnected the voter's ballot from the act of electing the electors, and the original intent of the "Presidential short ballot" was not to preclude a voter casting a mixed elector ballot. Note that the National Popular Vote mechanism does sever the connection between the voters and the electors; the electors are appointed in NPV states instead. It is however not active in 2020, and won't be unless enough states adopt it.

Arizona[37]	Arkansas	California[38]	Colorado	Connecticut
Delaware	Florida	Georgia	Hawaii	Idaho
Illinois	Iowa	Kansas	Kentucky	Louisiana
Maryland	Massachusetts	Michigan	Minnesota	Mississippi
Missouri	Nevada	New Jersey	North Dakota	Oregon
South Carolina	South Dakota	Texas	Vermont	Washington State
Washington DC	West Virginia	Wisconsin	Wyoming	

Figure 10.3 States whose election officials did not respond to author's question regarding mixed ballots in 2020

What voters are faced with here is one state which will count a mixed elector ballot under law, a few states that should count a mixed elector ballot, a few states that say they won't, and most that have no answer to the question.

The author suspects that after litigation, many if not most states will count the mixed elector ballots (whether that litigation happens before or after the seating of the electors is a different matter).[39]

You are the citizen and it is your vote.

---

[37] On election day 2020, after the first edition of this book was finalized, the author received a response from the Arizona Secretary of State's office indicating that a mixed elector ballot would be evaluated to determine "voter intent."

[38] The author has reasons to believe that California is likely to count a mixed elector ballot, it is covered in a footnote in Chapter 20.

[39] There are state by state variations that this book is unable to address. They will reveal themselves in due course. (I'm winging this to the best of my ability.) Nothing can be truly guaranteed except for Pennsylvania, assuming they leave the law in place. Note that paper ballots are preferable over the computer ballots, unless states add enough write-in spaces to the computer ballots.

But it would be *nice* if voters in each of the forty-nine jurisdictions cast a mixed elector ballot, so that the voter and the vote can be used for litigation to figure out if the mandatory straight ticket is truly mandatory.

It is vital for democracy.[40] We need to figure out how legitimate this democracy is. We are voting for the electors. Can we be forced to do so only by the mandatory straight ticket? Let state officials tell the voters directly why they must use the mandatory straight ticket.

The potential loss to you, the voter, is your normal straight-ticket vote for the presidential electors.

The potential gain is a more-rounded democracy and the satisfaction that you are no longer forced to cast a vote between only two unsatisfactory[41] choices.

---

[40] The ideal situation is, if a state refused to count mixed elector ballots then a voter advocacy group would fill the space and represent the mixed elector voters for no cost. This book can't control that outcome, but it is the ideal situation, and besides, there's nothing more American than suing your own state. (There is no potential financial gain, however, just the satisfaction of trying to improve American democracy.)

[41] This book is unable to guarantee satisfactory choices, just more unsatisfactory ones. But there's a lot more power for the voter in that. The American people can better balance out the parties'/candidates' unsatisfactory characteristics.

CHAPTER 11

Learning to Paint Your Ballot by Numbers

WHO ARE YOU AS A voter? Like, what are you politically?

One way of allocating the votes for presidential elector is to think of your political preferences as a proportional mix of the parties available.

So, for example, if you are:

20 percent Citrus Party
20 percent Pear Party
60 percent Apple Party

and a Pennsylvania voter with twenty votes for electors, you could express this political gradient with the proportion of four Citrus, four Pear and eight Apple votes for electors.

Remember, the American voter *creates the composition* of the Electoral College. So if you chose this method (and this method can be combined with others) you are creating the composition of your state's presidential elector delegation through the prism of your political preferences.

CHAPTER 12

Using Elector Order to Fine-Tune Your Ballot

IDEALLY, ALL PARTIES WOULD ORDER their presidential elector candidates. That is to say, if a voter were wanting to vote only some of the presidential elector candidates of the Pear or Apple parties, those parties should indicate the order in which voters should select their preference. With other voters following that order, it increases the chance of the top ranked elector winning office.

If you're not voting the full Pear Party Presidential Elector ticket, vote for candidates in this order:	
1	Bartlett Pear
2	Concorde Pear
3	Starkrimson Pear
4	Forelle Pear
5	Bosc Pear

Figure 12.1 Sample Pear Party Presidential Elector Ballot ordering

If you're not voting the full Apple Party Presidential Elector ticket, vote for candidates in this order:	
1	Ambrosia Apple
2	Fuji Apple
3	Gala Apple
4	Envy Apple
5	Honeycrisp Apple

Figure 12.2 Sample Apple Party Presidential Elector Ballot Ordering

This is important for all parties and independent candidates, but it's particularly key for minor parties and independents.

However voters can also use the order to fine-tune their political expression and strategic vote.

Consider the following tickets a voter can vote with the above Pear and Apple party orders:

Voter selects top three Apple Candidates, bottom two Pear Candidates	
1	Ambrosia Apple
2	Fuji Apple
3	Gala Apple
4	Forelle Pear
5	Bosc Pear

Figure 12.3 Sample Ballot Ordering, Top 3 Apples, Bottom 2 Pears

Voter selects top three Apple Candidates, top two Pear Candidates	
1	Ambrosia Apple
2	Fuji Apple
3	Gala Apple
4	Bartlett Pear
5	Concorde Pear

Figure 12.4 Sample Ballot Order, Top 3 Apples, Top 2 Pears

Voter selects bottom three Apple Candidates, bottom two Pear Candidates	
1	Gala Apple
2	Envy Apple
3	Honeycrisp Apple
4	Forelle Pear
5	Bosc Pear

Figure 12.5 Sample Ballot Ordering, Bottom 3 Apples, Bottom 2 Pears

Voter selects bottom three Apple Candidates, top two Pear Candidates	
1	Gala Apple
2	Envy Apple
3	Honeycrisp Apple
4	Bartlett Pear
5	Concorde Pear

Figure 12.6 Sample Ballot Ordering, Bottom 3 Apples, Top 2 Pears

These four tickets are all three Apple votes and two Pear votes. But because the voter is factoring in the suggested order, and assuming other voters are doing likewise, the voter is able to express a different democratic expression as well as submit a ballot with a different strategic intent.

This doesn't even factor in the secondary mandates a candidate for elector may have. Voters can mix and match electors who only have primary mandates ("inflexible" electors whose mandate we know will be carried out) and candidates with secondary mandates (who will flexibly adapt to circumstances of Stage Two.)

CHAPTER 13

2020 State-By-State Elector Autonomy

REGARDING THE 2020 ELECTION, THERE are thirty-five states whose voters can vote for electors with secondary mandates:[42]

Eighteen states with no restrictions on presidential elector autonomy/ states with elector candidates who can have secondary mandates:

Arkansas	Georgia	Idaho	Illinois
Kansas	Kentucky	Louisiana	Missouri
New Hampshire	New Jersey	New York	North Dakota
Pennsylvania	Rhode Island	South Dakota	Texas
Washington DC	West Virginia		

Figure 13.1 States with fully autonomous Presidential Electors

Sixteen states with a technical requirement to vote for the party nominee/"popular" vote winner, but no penalty for an autonomous elector and no mechanism for reversing their vote:

---

[42] "Faithless Elector State Laws," FairVote, July 7, 2020, https://www.fairvote.org/faithless_elector_state_laws.

Alabama	Alaska	Connecticut	Delaware
Florida	Hawaii	Maryland	Massachusetts
Mississippi	Ohio	Oregon	Tennessee
Vermont	Virginia	Wisconsin	Wyoming

Figure 13.2 States with de facto fully autonomous Presidential Electors

In three states, electors will be penalized (with fines/jail[43]) for their autonomy, but the vote will not be reversed:

California	New Mexico	South Carolina

Figure 13.3 States with irreversible but punishable
Presidential Elector autonomy

It is up to the elector if they are willing to accept the punishment in order to carry out the secondary mandate.

Voters in those thirty-five states above therefore can take into account an individual presidential elector candidate's preferences, particularly their secondary mandates, and enjoy a greater selection of choice on their ballots than the voters who live in states where the votes are reversible by the state and electors cannot have a secondary mandate.

List of states with a mechanism to prevent a vote from an autonomous elector, and therefore prevent an elector candidate from having a secondary mandate:

---

[43] In a personal belief, a candidate for presidential elector who expresses a willingness to be imprisoned to carry out a secondary mandate on behalf of the voter is worthy of a closer look. Thank you New Mexico for making this both awkward and interesting.

Arizona	Colorado	Indiana	Iowa
Maine	Michigan	Minnesota	Montana
Nebraska	Nevada	North Carolina	Oklahoma
Utah	Washington State		

Figure 13.4 States with non-autonomous Presidential Electors[44]

---

[44] Arizona, Colorado, and Utah technically bind the electors to the winner of the state's "popular" vote and not to the party nominee. How this works when a state doesn't have a "popular" vote because of voters casting mixed elector ballots is a fascinating question.

CHAPTER 14

The Benefits of Mixed Elector Ballots for Swing Voters and Voters with Minor Party or Independent Leanings

SWING VOTERS HAVE MUCH TO gain from the mixed elector ballot. When the quantity of voters casting mixed elector ballots exceeds the difference between the straight-ticket voters' top two, the split will be determined by the mixed elector voters.

Straight-ticket votes for party list A	2,002,453
Straight-ticket votes for party list B	2,000,079
Mixed elector ballots	6,050

Figure 14.1 Sample Election statistics with Mixed Elector Ballots

The distribution of elector seats here will be decided by the 6,050 mixed elector ballots.

Mixed elector ballots make it easier for a voter to cast a vote for a minor party or independent because voters still have the option to cast the rest of their ballots for a major party candidate. It's a different strategy and a different political expression. Casting all your elector votes for just one minor or independent party ticket is a lot for a voter—the mandatory straight tickets help the two major parties by discouraging votes for minor parties and independents.[45]

The mixed elector ballot creates a realizable goal for minor parties and independents. At this point having a plurality of Americans vote for a minor party or independent straight ticket is unlikely. However it is reasonable to believe that many Americans would be interested in balancing their ticket by casting a couple of their votes (or in a big state—several of their votes) for minor party elector candidates, independent elector candidates or unaffiliated elector candidates (discussed in Chapter 17.) This is impossible with the mandatory straight ticket—it's all or nothing. And since it is all or nothing, it's virtually impossible for a minor party/independent/unaffiliated elector candidate to be elected. But with mixed elector ballots, in combination with elector order from Chapter 12, it becomes much more likely that there would be elected minor party/independent/unaffiliated electors and therefore those views represented in Stage Two.

So much of the American political experience has become about preventing the election of presidential nominee A or nominee B. That is what the mandatory straight tickets force voters to do. With mixed elector ballots, voters have a much wider range of strategic decisions they can make.

---

[45] Not to mention the inability of the voter to make a proportional balance between the two major parties.

CHAPTER 15

The Problem with the Primaries

THE 2016 PRESIDENTIAL PRIMARIES WERE a fascinating democratic failure. Taking eight Republican nominees and four Democrats, and winnowing that list down, the primary process spent hundreds of millions of dollars and succeeded in choosing the combination of two presidential nominees Americans could collectively agree they wanted the least.

How did this happen? The primaries are not democratic events: voters are not able to participate in more than one primary (or put another way, the penalty of participating in a primary is the inability to participate in any other primary). Because of that, different groups of Americans participate in one primary or the other, and the results can be weirdly disbalanced. The disbalance is caused by multiple factors: voters of the extremes dominating primaries, voters of one party strategically picking a presidential nominee they think other people would like but really don't (so-called "electability"), and simple ballots without ranking in elections only requiring a plurality, which allow for candidates with relatively little support to win.

These problems cannot be evened out with the mandatory straight ticket, or the proposed National Popular Vote, which would do little more than change the nation from forty-nine state winner-takes-all to one nation winner-takes-all. (But it is still winner-takes-all; it builds on top of the mandatory straight ticket. It will carry over the mistakes and undemocratic problems of the primary process into roughly the same Stage One and State Two we have today.)[46]

Instead, voters casting mixed elector ballots with autonomous electors can even out the failures of the primaries. It offers voters the ability to reject the primary nominees for something else.

---

[46] Note that the National Popular Vote mechanism calculates the national popular vote by assessing the results of states with a "statewide popular" election. The NPV would not count results from Maine and Nebraska in their current configurations (as they aren't "statewide" elections) and any state with mixed elector ballots/whose voters cast any mixed elector ballots (as that wouldn't be a "popular" election.) The author asked National Popular Vote Inc. if just one voter casting a mixed elector ballot would be enough for the NPV to ignore the state, but received no response.

CHAPTER 16

Things the Electors Need to Fully Represent the Voters

THIS BOOK PROPOSES THAT THE most democratic way of interaction between voters and the presidential electors is for autonomous electors with a full relationship with voters. To achieve this, we will need:

- A greater period of time between the Stage One and Stage Two elections. One way of achieving this is to move the Stage One election to summer.
- Voters guides which include Presidential Elector candidate statements and primary/secondary mandate information.[47]
- Like any other elected official, presidential electors should be required to file ethics and campaign finance disclosures.
- Some of the activities of presidential electors need to be covered by public meetings laws.
- It is entirely reasonable to have primaries for presidential electors; indeed, that has happened in the past.

---

[47] Voters Guides are non-partisan documents prepared by state election officials with biographies and statements of all ballot listed candidates, plus information on referenda with arguments in favor and against. American democracy would benefit from them, but they are typically found only in western states. Those interested in seeing a sample can look at the California voters guide at https://voterguide.sos.ca.gov/

- A federal law for national electoral college procedures and operations—so that they are acting and communicating as a group.
- Security clearance under federal law.

CHAPTER 17

The Case for Unaffiliated Elector Candidates

AN UNAFFILIATED ELECTOR IS AN individual who is not connected to any presidential nominee nor are they running as a candidate for presidential elector for any party (in other words, they have no primary mandate).

Voters can evaluate unaffiliated elector candidates based on that candidate's merits, wisdom and preferences.

What that elector can and will do in Stage Two is a function of the above as well as the political dynamics of the other 537 electors.

The unaffiliated presidential elector is the original kind. All of the electors in the first Electoral College were chosen only for whom they were and had no pledges or bindings. The first Electoral College was a fascinating mix of America's founding fathers, American revolutionaries, and statesmen. It was because of their knowledge of each other and George Washington that lead them to the choice of Washington (see the list below.)

This book would encourage any American to consider running for the office of presidential elector as an unaffiliated candidate. The process of bringing democracy to the people begins with average Americans running for elector. The more choices Americans have on their ballots, the more they can effectively mix and match their votes for elector.

Electors of the Electoral College of February 4, 1789[48] who also:

...signed the Declaration of Independence in 1776.	Samuel Huntington of Connecticut George Walton of Georgia James Wilson of Pennsylvania Edward Rutledge of South Carolina
...signed the Articles of Confederation in 1778.	Samuel Huntington of Connecticut Francis Dana of Massachusetts Thomas Heyward Jr. of South Carolina
...signed the Constitution at the Constitutional Convention of 1787. *Note that these individuals would have certainly known George Washington personally, as he was president of this convention.	Gunning Bedford Jr. of Delaware David Brearley of New Jersey James Wilson of Pennsylvania Charles Cotesworth Pickney of South Carolina

Figure 17.1 Electors of the Electoral College of February 4, 1789 who were also at the signing of the Declaration of Independence, the Articles of Confederation, or the Constitution at the Constitutional Convention of 1787.

---

[48] Merrill Jensen, Lucy Trumbull Brown, Robert A. Becker, Gordon DenBoer, Charles D. Hagermann, *The Documentary History of the First Federal Elections, 1788-1790*, (Madison: University of Wisconsin Press, 1976.)

CHAPTER 18

The Dream: Creating the World's Finest Election System

WHEN VOTERS ARE CASTING MIXED elector ballots, they have a wider range of factors they can assess than just the popularity contest:

- setting their votes for elector as a proportion of their political preferences;
- factoring in the party's suggested order as a way to fine-tune that political expression and for strategic voting purposes;
- considering each elector candidate's secondary mandates such as that potential elector's wisdom and discretion, their secondary preferences, and the conditions under which they would vote for those secondary preferences, as well as characteristics the potential elector is looking for in a president and vice president;
- any unaffiliated presidential elector candidates (those with no connection to a presidential ticket/no primary mandate);
- as well as the popularity contest.

The dream is that this would be how all voters would vote. (As well as lobby their elected electors after Stage One but before Stage Two.) But it doesn't take that many voters using this process to influence the states' Electoral College delegations and in doing so, significantly democratize it.

Remember, in Stage One we *create the composition* of the Electoral College.

The goal of this system is not the selection of an individual for president Americans like the most. In such a polarized nation that is impossible.[49]

Instead, the goal is to select an individual for president that Americans can agree *we dislike the least.*

We can do that by creating an Electoral College which is a precise, balanced reflection of the American voters' political desires.

The book would believe that voters actively using mixed elector ballots might create an Electoral College with a composition like:

Major Party A Electors	250
Major Party B Electors	250
Minor Party/Independent/Unaffiliated Electors	38

Figure 18.1 Potential Electoral College Results with wide use of Mixed Elector Ballots

...in which case the balance of power between the two major parties is held by the 38 minor party/independent/unaffiliated electors. That is a nightmare for the two major parties and their winner-takes-all preferences, but it would be a more democratic outcome, and it reduces the power of the parties in favor of the voters.

What might happen in the scenario above? That is dependent on the electors the voters have chosen. It is by scrutinizing the candidates for elector that we can elect electors who would most effectively represent us in Stage Two. That is their job. The more electors that have secondary mandates, the more the results will match the combined political expression Americans made in Stage One.

---

[49] The two main parties put a lot of money every election cycle to ensure that you hate either one candidate or the other. Polarization is a key part of their campaign strategy. Facing voters with mixed elector ballots, that strategy is less useful.

CHAPTER 19

What Maine and Nebraska Do

MAINE (FOUR ELECTORS) AND NEBRASKA (five electors) use a presidential elector district system (which have the same borders as the states' Congressional districts).

In Maine that means voters are in either one of two presidential elector districts and cast one vote each.

In Nebraska voters are in one of three presidential elector districts and cast one vote each.

Each state has two remaining electors. These are chosen by the winner of the statewide "popular" vote.

This book argues that these four electors are not democratically elected. They are appointed by the state legislature through a random criteria. (One which on the surface appears to be democratic in some way, but really isn't.)

When other states have used presidential elector districts (New York and Michigan in the nineteenth century) all the presidential electors were democratically elected in districts.

The Maine and Nebraska systems can be called "winner-takes-most." It is unclear to the author what problem this system is trying to solve.[50]

In any case, since voters in Maine and Nebraska are stuck in one-person

---

[50] At least in the case of Nebraska, it would appear to be a political compromise internal to that state's politics.

presidential elector districts, there is no ability to mix and match votes. Given this book's goal to maximize the power of the voters, it would recommend that those states abandon their part elected/part appointed Presidential Electors for statewide elections with mixed elector ballots.[51]

---

[51] Maine is currently pioneering the use of ranked choice voting, which is certainly a more democratic system than one choice ballots. Ranked choice voting in combination with a statewide election for electors and mixed elector ballots would be a powerfully precise system.

CHAPTER 20

On California and Small States

THIS BOOK DOES NOT ADVOCATE the removal of the presidential elector straight-ticket device, only that it not be mandatory.

Casting fifty-five mixed elector votes is unquestionably a task. Whether you are painting by number, and/or assessing the primary and secondary mandates of each elector candidate, filling that ballot out will take time.

Even if there should exist a website to help you do this process (something like isidewith.com or procon.org) in which you take a questionnaire and it prepares the list of fifty-five electors for you that you could submit as your ballot, it will take some time to answer the questions for the algorithm to create the ballot. (Such a website would be quite helpful.)

You are the citizen; it is your vote.

You can put as little or as much time you want into voting.

But fifty-five votes offers an extraordinary universe of possibilities for strategic voting and expressing a political preference.

With 55 votes and 275 ballot-listed candidates for presidential elector, a 2016 California voter would have had 3.4x10^58 combinations with a mixed elector ballot.[52]

---

[52] This is simplified, leaving out the write-ins and the American Independent Party electors. There were technically 605 elector candidates on the ballot when they are all included:. That yields 6.2x10^78 possible combinations.

But in reality voters were stuck with five ballot-listed straight tickets.[53]

—⁂—

The focus on California[54] as a special case is because with so many elector votes California voters would enjoy an unbelievable variety of possible political expressions. It is something of a dream to imagine how California voters (as any state's voters) would experiment with so many votes and the granularity that comes with that. A California voter concerned about the election of presidential nominee A or B but still wanting to balance their vote with non-major party candidates could give 40 to major party elector candidates and 15 votes to minor/independent/unaffiliated elector candidates. The risk to the voter is that 15 of the disliked major party presidential nominee's electors may win office due to their vote (a small chance in such a big state.)

Voters in small states with 3 electors don't have the advantage of all the granularity the big state voters enjoy but they get a different advantage: because the states are small, the margins between the elector candidates' results are smaller. So while voters have fewer choices than the big states, and a bigger risk of a disfavored elector winning office due to their vote, the smaller margin between vote totals makes it more likely that a voter would cause a mixed electoral result which matches their ballot.

In that way mixed elector ballots with autonomous electors balance small state and large state voters: voters in big states like California enjoy a lot of

---

[53] This book might argue that of the 3.4x10^58 combinations lost, the remaining five are among the worst.

[54] The author is optimistic about California counting mixed elector ballots in 2020. California Election Code ELEC § 6902 establishes the connection between the voters and the electors: "At the general election in each leap year, or at any other time as may be prescribed by the laws of the United States, there shall be chosen by the voters of the state as many electors of President and Vice President of the United States as the state is then entitled to."

choices in filling out their ballots. Each big state voter has a small influence over a large part of the electoral college. Small state voters have fewer choices but small state voters have a higher chance of influencing the election result, so they have a large influence on a small part of the electoral college.

CHAPTER 21

The Casino

A funny thing happens every four years in America.

The people of the United States enter into a casino with fifty-one roulette wheels.[55] At which point they gather around their states' wheel and start screaming at each other:

"AS A TEXAS VOTER, I AM PLACING ALL THIRTY-EIGHT OF MY CHIPS ON RED TO KEEP BLUE FROM WINNING TEXAS!"

"I'M FROM ILLINOIS, AND I AM PUTTING ALL TWENTY OF MY CHIPS ON BLUE TO KEEP RED FROM WINNING ILLINOIS."

"THIS IS NEW MEXICO'S WHEEL, AND I AM PUTTING ALL FIVE OF MY CHIPS ON YELLOW BECAUSE OF HOW MUCH I HATE THIS CASINO."

With all the yelling going on, it goes unnoticed that the roulette wheels only have a few solid color spaces. The rest of the wheel is empty space.

But the truth is, we've been using these roulette wheels for nearly two centuries, and if the dealer picks up the wheel and flips it over, those empty spaces have trillions of color and number combinations we can use that haven't been seen in decades.

All we need to do is ask the dealers to flip the wheels over and in doing so, reclaim power that is rightfully ours.

---

[55] Which would be one big wheel under the National Popular Vote. That's its only change.

CHAPTER 22

We Are Not Having a Free and Fair Election

WHILE THERE WERE MANY, MANY reasons for why elections in East Germany weren't "free and fair," this book does not consider elections for presidential elector via the mandatory straight tickets as meeting the criteria for a "free and fair" election:

1. The names of the candidates voters are voting for are hidden.
2. In their place are the names of people voters are not voting for.
3. Voters are not told that their vote is being multiplied and in reality they are casting multiple votes simultaneously.
4. Voters are not told nor are provided with ballots that would allow them to split their multiple votes. Even in Pennsylvania, which actually has a decades-old law allowing for mixed votes, voters aren't told it's possible to split their votes.
5. This book would argue that, absent a law which specifically requires that voters can only vote for candidates for elector by straight-ticket device, a voter in any of the forty-nine affected jurisdictions should be able to do this. Nevertheless, some states have told this author that voters not using the state printed ballot, and its mandatory straight-ticket devices, would not have their votes counted.
6. Even though voters are electing the electors, binding laws bind the

electors to the party's nominee and hinder the ability of the voters to have a relationship with the electors.

7. And while it is not directly related to the mandatory straight ticket, the severity of the mandatory straight ticket is all the more when combined with ballot access laws, which make it difficult for independents and minor parties to get on state ballots.

CHAPTER 23

Conclusion

It's interesting that political scientists over the last century have looked at the mandatory straight ticket and thought it was inoffensive and convenient.

This book looks at it as democracy denied. A purposeful rigging of the election to leave voters with as few choices as possible to maximize the power of the two major political parties at the expense of voters.

It's a curious position to be in to question a century's worth of American elections, and conclude that they were not truly democratic events.

But I believe that when voters understand how the mandatory straight ticket works, see how ballots of the past looked and how this system could be more democratic, they will agree that the mandatory straight ticket is democracy denied. A century-long scam on the American voter.

Even if you are content to use the straight ticket when you vote for presidential elector, use it with the knowledge that you are casting multiple votes simultaneously.

While there are multiple winner-takes-all mechanisms, the key mechanism is found on your ballot, preventing your mixing and matching of your votes.

This transfer of power from your ballot to the major parties is happening to you personally.

APPENDIX A

Best Known Year in Which a State First Adopted the Mandatory Straight Ticket[56]

Alabama 1976
Arizona 1916 (except Graham County, 1920)
Arkansas 1964
California 1940
Colorado 1944
Connecticut 1936
Delaware 1944
Florida 1952
Georgia 1968
Idaho 1944
Illinois 1928

---

[56] This section is thanks to Richard Winger from Ballot Access News (http://ballot-access.org/) It was determined by looking at election statistics and when the results for Presidential Elector were uniform for all the Electors of one party. In some instances, the year was determined by looking at old ballots. Alaska, Hawaii, and DC always had the mandatory straight ticket.

Indiana 1940
Iowa 1920
Kansas 1936
Kentucky 1944
Louisiana 1980
Maine either 1952, 1956, or 1960
Maryland 1940

Massachusetts 1932
Michigan 1932
Minnesota 1904
Mississippi 1984
Missouri 1936
Montana 1936
Nebraska 1920
Nevada 1940
New Hampshire 1928
New Jersey 1944
New Mexico 1956
New York 1940
North Carolina 1936
North Dakota 1932
Ohio 1932
Oklahoma 1928
Oregon 1928

Pennsylvania 1932
Rhode Island 1940
South Carolina 1984
South Dakota 1932
Tennessee 1936
Texas 1948
Utah 1948
Vermont 1980
Virginia 1924
Washington 1936
West Virginia 1956
Wisconsin 1928
Wyoming 1928

Figure A.1 Year States Adopted Mandatory Straight Ticket

Apropos of Nothing, Dealing with the Money Problem

Candidate ballot order gets less attention than it deserves. Candidates at the top of the ballot have a natural advantage than those at the bottom. It was mentioned that Ohio rotates its ballot order so every candidate has an equal chance at being at the top. It really is an excellent system.

Some states put the candidate whose party won a last election at the top, giving a natural advantage to the strongest party in the state.

Some states do it by lottery.

Others do it alphabetically.

The proposal here is that they do it by the amount of money involved. The more candidates spend or have spent on their behalf, the *lower* on the ballot they are. It balances out the campaign spending by giving an advantage to those who had the least amount of money in their campaigns. By including "dark" money (money spent on behalf of the candidate, but not actually raised by the candidate) that would also discourage some of this behavior.

Candidates for State Senate, District 5		Money raised and spent by candidate plus spent on behalf of candidate
Sour Grapefruit	Citrus	$71,055
Gala Apple[57]	Apple	$121,912
Taylor Gold	Pear	$207,011

Figure B.1 Sample Money Revealing Ballot

This is a general section of this book meant to deal with a campaign finance problem that has been bothering many Americans. The money-revealing ballot can be used for a presidential elector with variation of the above.

---

[57] Gala Apple is being a bad apple, being listed on the ballot twice for two different offices: state senator and presidential elector. In most states, an individual is only allowed to hold one office at a time, and is only allowed to run for one office at a time. But because presidential elector is not listed on the ballot, people forget they're candidates for a public office. In 2016 numerous individuals in a variety of states were candidates for presidential elector and another office simultaneously, as well as held another office at the same time as presidential elector. The most egregious case was Florida, which in 2016 had eleven presidential electors who were already holding another office (including Attorney General and state legislature). The error is not harmless, but it is unintentional. The author of this book has been a candidate for presidential elector at the same time he was a candidate for another office. Ohio voters will be relieved to know that he lost both

APPENDIX C
Random state ballots

1908 Ohio Ballot[58]

The 1908 Ohio ballot has a special place for me because it was the first Mixed Elector Ballot I had seen. This ballot features full ballot straight ticket devices and this particular sample from the Akron Beacon Journal shows that paper's then Republican leanings.

With 136 Candidates for Presidential Elector, a 1908 Ohio voter had 6.3×10^{25} different ways of casting their 23 votes.

---

[58] "Fac-simile of ballot and instructions how to vote," *The Akron Beacon Journal* (Akron, Ohio), October 31, 1908, Page 12.

FAC-SIMILE OF BALLOT AND INSTRUCTIONS HOW TO VOTE

| PROPOSED AMENDMENTS | REPUBLICAN TICKET. | DEMOCRATIC TICKET. | SOCIALIST TICKET | PROHIBITION TICKET | INDEPENDENCE TICKET | PEOPLE'S PARTY TICKET | SOCIALIST LABOR TICKET | DIRECT LEGISLATION TICKET |

Figure C.1 1908 Ohio Ballot

1908 Nebraska[59]

The 1908 Nebraska features multiple straight tickets, one set in the upper left hand corner for the full ballot, and a second set only for Presidential Electors. Note that this ballot does not have the names of the Presidential Nominees (since they aren't candidates on the ballot there is no need for them to appear on the ballot.)

With 28 candidates for Elector, a 1908 Nebraska voter had 3,108,105 different ways of voting their 8 votes.

---

[59] *The Alliance Herald.* (Alliance, Box Butte County, Nebraska.), October 29, 1908, Chronicling America: Historic American Newspapers. Library of Congress, https://chroniclingamerica.loc.gov/lccn/2010270501/1908-10-29/ed-1/seq-6/

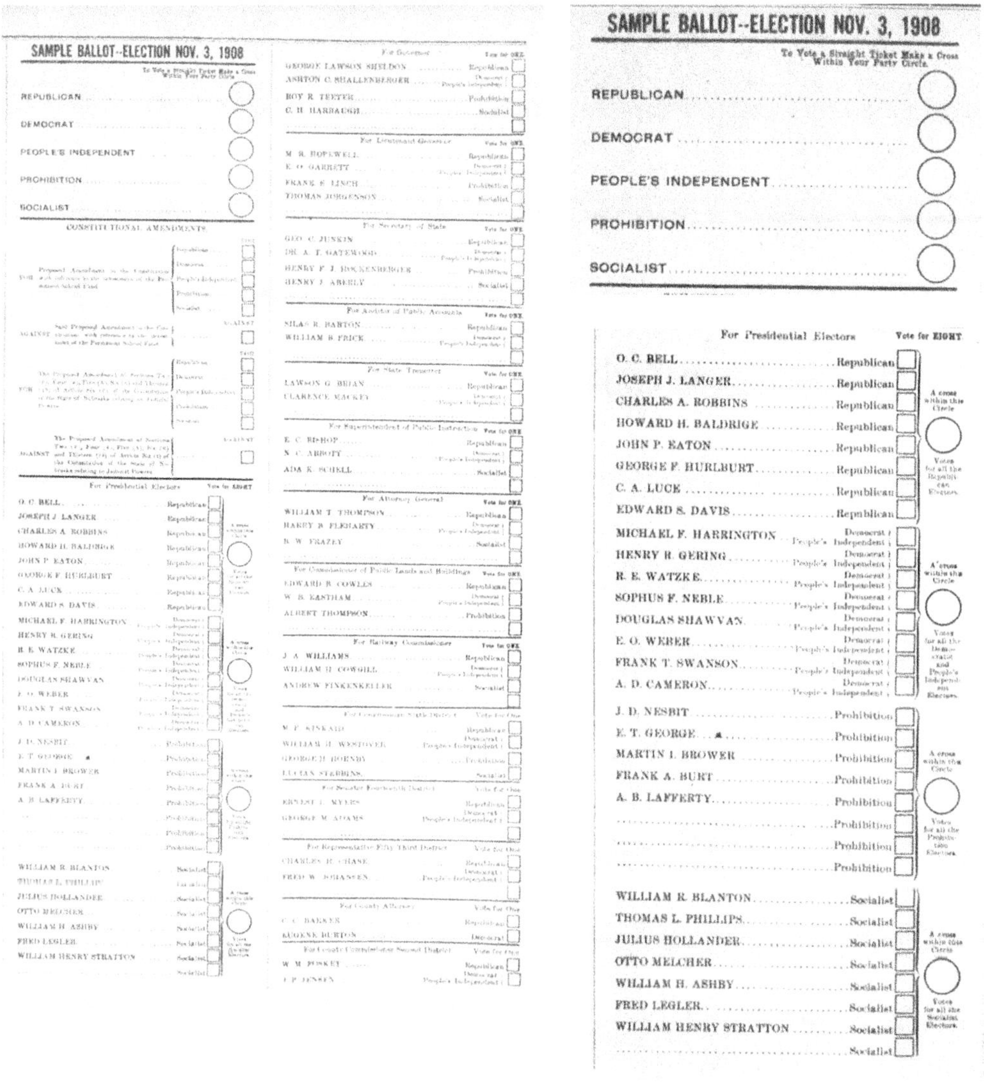

SAMPLE BALLOT--ELECTION NOV. 3, 1908

To Vote a Straight Ticket Make a Cross Within Your Party Circle.

REPUBLICAN ....

DEMOCRAT ....

PEOPLE'S INDEPENDENT ....

PROHIBITION ....

SOCIALIST ....

For Presidential Electors — Vote for EIGHT

O. C. BELL .... Republican
JOSEPH J. LANGER .... Republican
CHARLES A. ROBBINS .... Republican
HOWARD H. BALDRIGE .... Republican
JOHN P. EATON .... Republican
GEORGE F. HURLBURT .... Republican
C. A. LUCE .... Republican
EDWARD S. DAVIS .... Republican

A cross within this Circle Votes for all the Republican Electors.

MICHAEL F. HARRINGTON .... Democrat / People's Independent
HENRY R. GERING .... Democrat / People's Independent
R. E. WATZKE .... Democrat / People's Independent
SOPHUS F. NEBLE .... Democrat / People's Independent
DOUGLAS SHAWVAN .... Democrat / People's Independent
E. O. WEBER .... Democrat / People's Independent
FRANK T. SWANSON .... Democrat / People's Independent
A. D. CAMERON .... Democrat / People's Independent

A cross within this Circle Votes for all the Democratic and People's Independent Electors.

J. D. NESBIT .... Prohibition
E. T. GEORGE .... Prohibition
MARTIN I. BROWER .... Prohibition
FRANK A. BURT .... Prohibition
A. B. LAFFERTY .... Prohibition
.... Prohibition
.... Prohibition
.... Prohibition

A cross within the Circle Votes for all the Prohibition Electors.

WILLIAM R. BLANTON .... Socialist
THOMAS L. PHILLIPS .... Socialist
JULIUS HOLLANDER .... Socialist
OTTO MELCHER .... Socialist
WILLIAM H. ASHBY .... Socialist
FRED LEGLER .... Socialist
WILLIAM HENRY STRATTON .... Socialist
.... Socialist

A cross within this Circle Votes for all the Socialist Electors.

Figure C.2 1908 Nebraska Ballot with close-ups

1940 Utah[60]

The 1940 Utah featured 16 candidates for Presidential Elector, giving Utah voters 1820 different ways to cast their 4 votes.

On a side note, Ada Williams Quinn, the candidate for Governor under the "A Business Woman for Governor" label founded an apron making factory which employed widows in Ogden, Utah. At its height it employed 200 workers. Readers interested in more information on her life can find it at https://historytogo.utah.gov/quinn-ada/

____

[60] "Sample Ballot," *Bear River Valley Leader,* (Tremonton City, Utah), October 31, 1940, Page 3

SAMPLE BALLOT

DEMOCRATIC	REPUBLICAN	COMMUNIST PARTY OF UTAH	SOCIALIST	A BUSINESS WOMAN FOR GOVERNOR	
President FRANKLIN D. ROOSEVELT	President WENDELL L. WILLKIE	President EARL BROWDER	President NORMAN THOMAS	President	President
Vice-President HENRY A. WALLACE	Vice-President CHARLES L. McNARY	Vice-President JAMES W. FORD	Vice-President MAYNARD C. KRUEGER	Vice-President	Vice-President
For Presidential Electors MRS. GEO. S. BALLIF	For Presidential Electors MRS. B. L. ASHBY	For Presidential Electors DAVID DOUGLAS, JR.	For Presidential Electors ISABEL ADAMSON	For Presidential Electors	For Presidential Electors
SOPHUS BEETLESON	S. MARION BLISS	MARGUERITE H. FOREST	J. D. DEFRIEZ		
JOSEPH JENSEN	CLARENCE DAHL	WILLIAM MATHRUS	WM. J. McCONNELL		
OSCAR W. McCONKIE	JOHN W. GUILD	HYRUM JAMES WOOLMAN	EMIL MUNZ		
For United States Senator ABE MURDOCK	For United States Senator CHILD T. FARNSWORTH JR.	For United States Senator	For United States Senator	For United States Senator	For United States Senator
For Representative in Congress WALTER K. GRANGER	For Representative in Congress LeROY B. YOUNG	For Representative in Congress	For Representative in Congress	For Representative in Congress	For Representative in Congress
For Justice of Supreme Court EUGENE E. PRATT	For Justice of Supreme Court JOSEPH F. EVANS	For Justice of Supreme Court	For Justice of Supreme Court	For Justice of Supreme Court	For Justice of Supreme Court
For Governor HERBERT B. MAW	For Governor DON B. COLTON	For Governor	For Governor	For Governor ADA WILLIAMS QUINN	For Governor
For Secretary of State E. E. MONSON	For Secretary of State LLOYD RILEY	For Secretary of State	For Secretary of State	For Secretary of State	For Secretary of State
For State Auditor REESE M. REESE	For State Auditor WALTER A. DAY	For State Auditor	For State Auditor	For State Auditor	For State Auditor
For State Treasurer OLIVER G. ELLIS	For State Treasurer O. EARL THOMAS	For State Treasurer	For State Treasurer	For State Treasurer	For State Treasurer
For Attorney General GROVER A. GILES	For Attorney General MELVIN C. HARRIS	For Attorney General	For Attorney General	For Attorney General	For Attorney General
For State Supt. of Public Instruction CHARLES H. SKIDMORE	For State Supt. of Public Instruction CALVIN S. SMITH	For State Supt. of Public Instruction	For State Supt. of Public Instruction	For State Supt. of Public Instruction	For State Supt. of Public Instruction
For District Judge LEWIS JONES	For District Judge CHARLES W. DUNN	For District Judge	For District Judge	For District Judge	For District Judge
For District Attorney GEORGE D. PRESTON	For District Attorney BENJAMIN C. CALL	For District Attorney	For District Attorney	For District Attorney	For District Attorney
For State Senator AREL S. RICH	For State Senator ALBERT E. HOLMGREN	For State Senator	For State Senator	For State Senator	For State Senator
For State Representative Dist. No. 2 DAVID E. WALDRON	For State Representative Dist. No. 2 CLIFTON G. M. KERR	For State Representative Dist. No. 2	For State Representative Dist. No. 2	For State Representative Dist. No. 2	For State Representative Dist. No. 2
For County Commissioner, 4-Year Term OSEY JENSON	For County Commissioner, 4-Year Term E. J. HOLMGREN	For County Commissioner, 4-Year Term	For County Commissioner, 4-Year Term	For County Commissioner, 4-Year Term	For County Commissioner, 4-Year Term
For County Commissioner, 2-Year Term JOSEPH A. NIELSEN	For County Commissioner, 2-Year Term NOBLE HUNSAKER	For County Commissioner, 2-Year Term	For County Commissioner, 2-Year Term	For County Commissioner, 2-Year Term	For County Commissioner, 2-Year Term
For County Attorney MARRINER M. MORRISON	For County Attorney WALTER G. MANN	For County Attorney	For County Attorney	For County Attorney	For County Attorney

CONSTITUTIONAL AMENDMENT—Liability of Stockholders of Banks

A Joint Resolution Proposing to Amend Section 18, Article XII, of the Constitution of the State of Utah, Relating to Liability of Stockholders of Banks

YES ☐   NO ☐

STATE OF UTAH
County of Box Elder

I, C. HENRY NIELSEN, County Clerk in and for the County of Box Elder, in the State of Utah, do hereby certify that the foregoing is a full, true and correct copy of the names of all the candidates for offices to be nominated, for the General Election to be held on Tuesday, November 5th, A. D. 1940, as appears on file in my office.

In Witness Whereof, I have hereunto set my hand and affixed my official seal this 28th day of October, A. D. 1940.

(SEAL)
     C. HENRY NIELSEN,
     County Clerk

Figure C.3 1940 Utah Ballot

1892 California[61]

Like the 1908 Nebraska, the 1892 California does not have the names of the Presidential Nominees on the ballot.

It had no straight ticket devices.

With 36 candidates for Presidential Elector, voters in 1892 California had 94,143,280 different ways of casting their 9 votes.

---

[61] *The Morning Call,* (San Francisco, California), October 28, 1892, Chronicling America: Historic American Newspapers, Library of Congress, https://chroniclingamerica.loc.gov/lccn/sn94052989/1892-10-28/ed-1/seq-8/

GENERAL TICKET.

4th Congressional District.

25th Senatorial District.   45th Assembly District.

City and County of San Francisco.

GENERAL TICKET.

4th Congressional District.

23d Senatorial District.   39th Assembly District.

City and County of San Francisco.

Figure C.4 1892 California Ballot

1908 Washington State[62]

The 1908 Washington ballot did not list the names of the Presidential Nominees but did have full ballot straight tickets.

With 25 candidates for Presidential Elector, a Washington voter in 1908 had 53,130 ways of casting their 5 votes.

---

[62] *The Seattle Star,* (Seattle, Washington), October 30, 1908

Figure C.5 1908 Washington State Ballot with close-up

1896 Kentucky[63]

The 1896 Kentucky had no straight ticket devices nor did it have the names of the Presidential Nominees.

With 52 candidates for Presidential Elector, a voter in 1896 Kentucky had 635 million (635,013,559,600) different ways of casting their 13 votes.

---

[63] *The Breckenridge News,* (Cloverport, Kentucky), October 21,1896, Chronicling America: Historic American Newspapers, Library of Congress, https:// chroniclingamerica.loc.gov/lccn/sn86069309/1896-10-21/ed-1/seq-4/

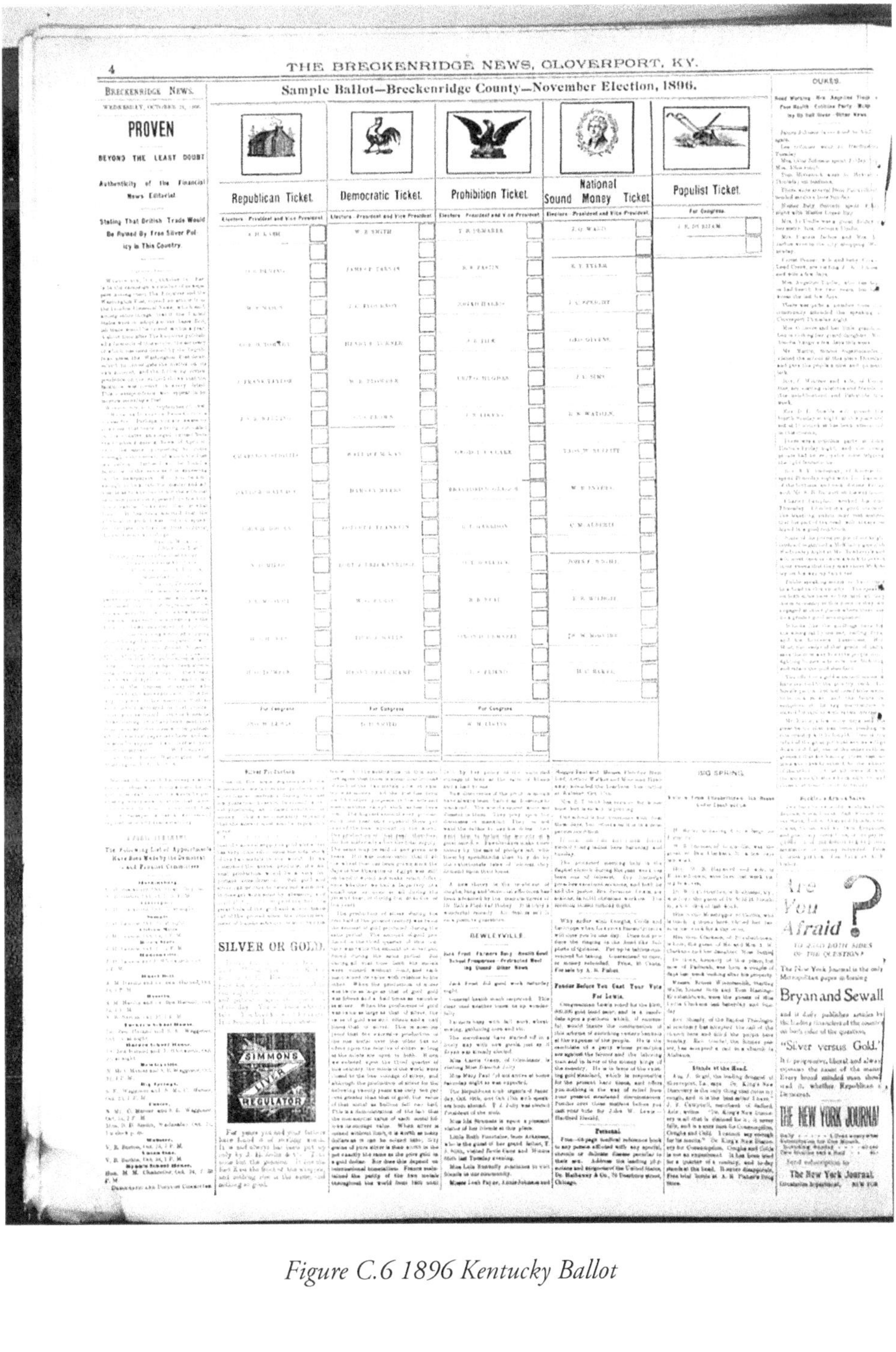
4 THE BRECKENRIDGE NEWS, CLOVERPORT, KY.

Sample Ballot—Breckenridge County—November Election, 1896.

Republican Ticket.

Democratic Ticket.

Prohibition Ticket.

National Sound Money Ticket

Populist Ticket.

PROVEN

BEYOND THE LEAST DOUBT

Authenticity of the Financial News Editorial

Stating That British Trade Would Be Ruined By Free Silver Policy in This Country.

SILVER OR GOLD.

SIMMONS LIVER REGULATOR

DUKES.

BIG SPRING.

BEWLEYVILLE.

Are You Afraid?

Bryan and Sewall

"Silver versus Gold."

THE NEW YORK JOURNAL

Figure C.6 1896 Kentucky Ballot

1932 North Carolina[64]

The 1932 North Carolina had full ballot straight tickets but did not have the names of the Presidential Nominees.

As shown by the ballot, two candidates of each party for Elector were statewide and the other 11 were in Presidential Elector districts which overlapped with Congressional districts. However, all voters statewide voted for all 13 (hypothetically the candidate for Elector lived in the district for which they were running.) This method is still used in some states today.

Prior to 1932 North Carolina did not have state printed ballots (it was one of the last states to adopt the state printed "Australian ballot.") After this election North Carolina switched to the mandatory straight ticket, so this is the only election in which North Carolina voters would have experienced a state printed Mixed Elector Ballot.

While most Elector candidates were in districts, it does not appear that precluded a voter for voting for multiple candidates from one district, so in effect it's just a normal Mixed Elector Ballot.

With 39 candidates for Presidential Elector, a North Carolina voter in 1932 would have had 8 billion (8,122,425,444) different ways of voting for 13 Electors.

---

[64] *Asheville Citizen-Times,* (Asheville, North Carolina), November 6, 1932, Page 11

<table>
<tr><td>

DEMOCRATIC
FOR A STRAIGHT TICKET

◯

MARK WITHIN THIS CIRCLE

For Electors at Large
J. CRAWFORD BIGGS
A. HALL JOHNSTON

For District Electors
First Congressional District:
THAD EURE

Second Congressional District:
E. R. TYLER

Third Congressional District:
W. W. PEARSALL

Fourth Congressional District:
HAROLD D. COOLEY

Fifth Congressional District:
FRED S. HUTCHINS

Sixth Congressional District:
COOPER E. HALL

Seventh Congressional District:
D. M. STRINGFIELD

Eighth Congressional District:
ROWLAND S. PRUETT

Ninth Congressional District:
B. F. WILLIAMS

Tenth Congressional District:
JOHN A. McRAE

Eleventh Congressional District:
PHILLIP C. COCKE

</td><td>

REPUBLICAN
FOR A STRAIGHT TICKET

◯

MARK WITHIN THIS CIRCLE

For Electors at Large
WALTER R. CHAMBERS
STUART W. CRAMER

For District Electors
First Congressional District:
PETER D. BURGESS

Second Congressional District:
W. F. OUTLAND

Third Congressional District:
GRAHAM W. DUNCAN

Fourth Congressional District:
SAM J. MORRIS

Fifth Congressional District:
E. A. TILLEY

Sixth Congressional District:
HORACE HAYWORTH

Seventh Congressional District:
LOUIS GOODMAN

Eighth Congressional District:
J. MACK BROWN

Ninth Congressional District:
G. W. KLUTZ

Tenth Congressional District:
R. H. SHUFORD

Eleventh Congressional District:
JAMES F. BARRETT

</td><td>

SOCIALIST
FOR A STRAIGHT TICKET

◯

MARK WITHIN THIS CIRCLE

For Electors at Large
F. A. SHOE
L. H. WILLIAMSON

For District Electors
First Congressional District:
W. K. SAUNDERS

Second Congressional District:
C. H. HAMLIN

Third Congressional District:
J. B. McDANIEL

Fourth Congressional District:
G. O. MUDGE

Fifth Congressional District:
A. T. HANES

Sixth Congressional District:
W. M. WEATHERLY

Seventh Congressional District:
C. E. DENNING

Eighth Congressional District:
M. P. BLAIR

Ninth Congressional District:
W. E. HENNESSEE

Tenth Congressional District:
A. T. MORETZ

Eleventh Congressional District:
F. K. GARDNER

</td></tr>
</table>

Figure C.7 1932 North Carolina Ballot

1908 Pennsylvania[65]

The 1908 Pennsylvania had a full ballot straight ticket as well as straight tickets for the Presidential Electors.

In the right hand column is a write-in space for Presidential Electors which contained a full 34 blanks. This is the space in which Pennsylvania voters today should be able to cast a Mixed Elector Ballot. (If it's there.)

With 204 candidates for Elector a Pennsylvania voter in 1908 had 6.1x10^38 different ways of casting their 34 votes.

____

[65] "Sample Ballot" Mount Carmel Item, (Mount Carmel, Pennsylvania), October 30, 1908

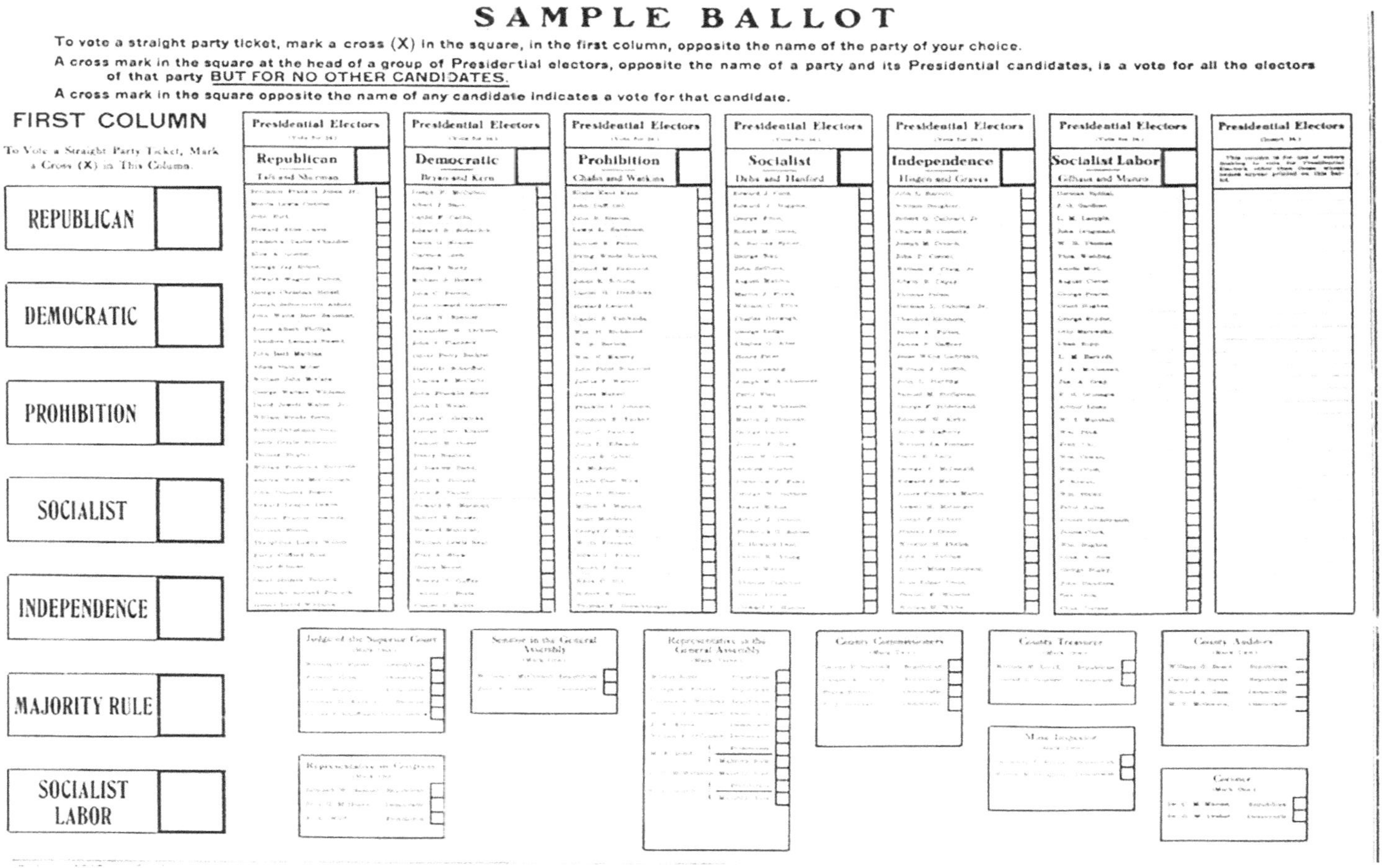

SAMPLE BALLOT

To vote a straight party ticket, mark a cross (X) in the square, in the first column, opposite the name of the party of your choice.

A cross mark in the square at the head of a group of Presidential electors, opposite the name of a party and its Presidential candidates, is a vote for all the electors of that party BUT FOR NO OTHER CANDIDATES.

A cross mark in the square opposite the name of any candidate indicates a vote for that candidate.

FIRST COLUMN

To Vote a Straight Party Ticket, Mark a Cross (X) in This Column.

REPUBLICAN

DEMOCRATIC

PROHIBITION

SOCIALIST

INDEPENDENCE

MAJORITY RULE

SOCIALIST LABOR

Presidential Electors — Republican — Taft and Sherman

Presidential Electors — Democratic — Bryan and Kern

Presidential Electors — Prohibition — Chafin and Watkins

Presidential Electors — Socialist — Debs and Hanford

Presidential Electors — Independence — Hisgen and Graves

Presidential Electors — Socialist Labor — Gillhaus and Munro

Presidential Electors

Judge of the Superior Court

Senator in the General Assembly

Representative in the General Assembly

County Commissioners

County Treasurer

County Auditors

Representative in Congress

Mine Inspector

Coroner

Figure C.8 1908 Pennsylvania Ballot

1940 Texas[66]

This 1940 Texas ballot is in a curious advertisement by county Democrats against the re-election of Roosevelt for a 3rd term (arguing that an individual should not be President for more than two terms.) It also makes a race-baiting argument against voting for Roosevelt.

Like the 1896 West Virginia elsewhere in this book, a voter crossed out the tickets they didn't want. Here the instructions are to cross out all the Electors except the Republicans but cross out all the local offices except the Democrats.

With 100 candidates a voter in 1940 Texas had 2.4x10^22 ways of voting their 23 voters for Elector.

---

[66] "How to vote for Wendell L. Willkie," *The Vernon Daily Record,* (Vernon Texas), November 2, 1940, Page 5.

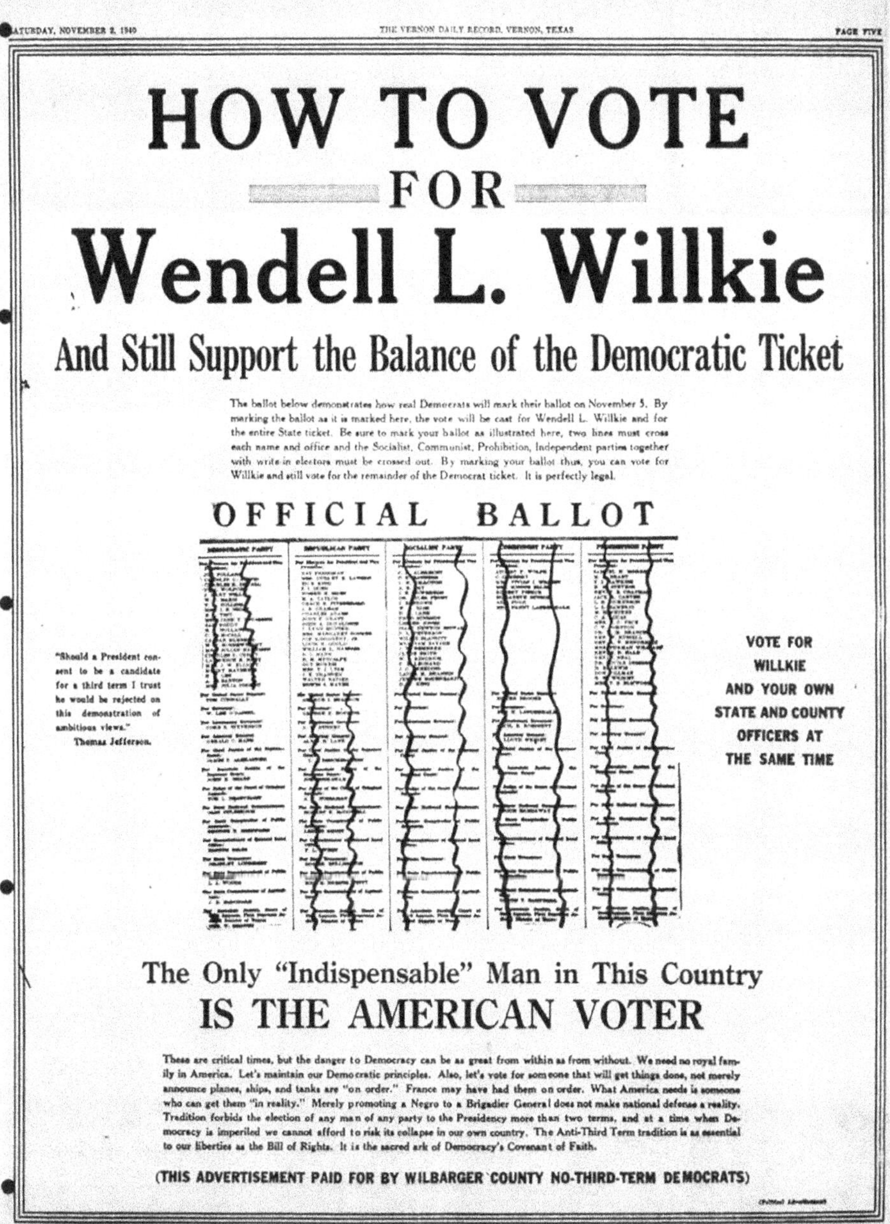

Figure C.9 Advertisement for Wendell Willkie, 1940 Texas Ballot

1904 Illinois[67]

This 1904 Illinois featured full ballot straight ticket devices.

With 189 candidates an Illinois voter in 1904 would have had 3.8x10^32 different ways of voting their 27 votes for Presidential Elector.

---

[67] "Sample Ballot, Election Tuesday, November 6, 1904," *Nashville Journal,* (Nashville, Illinois), November 3, 1904.

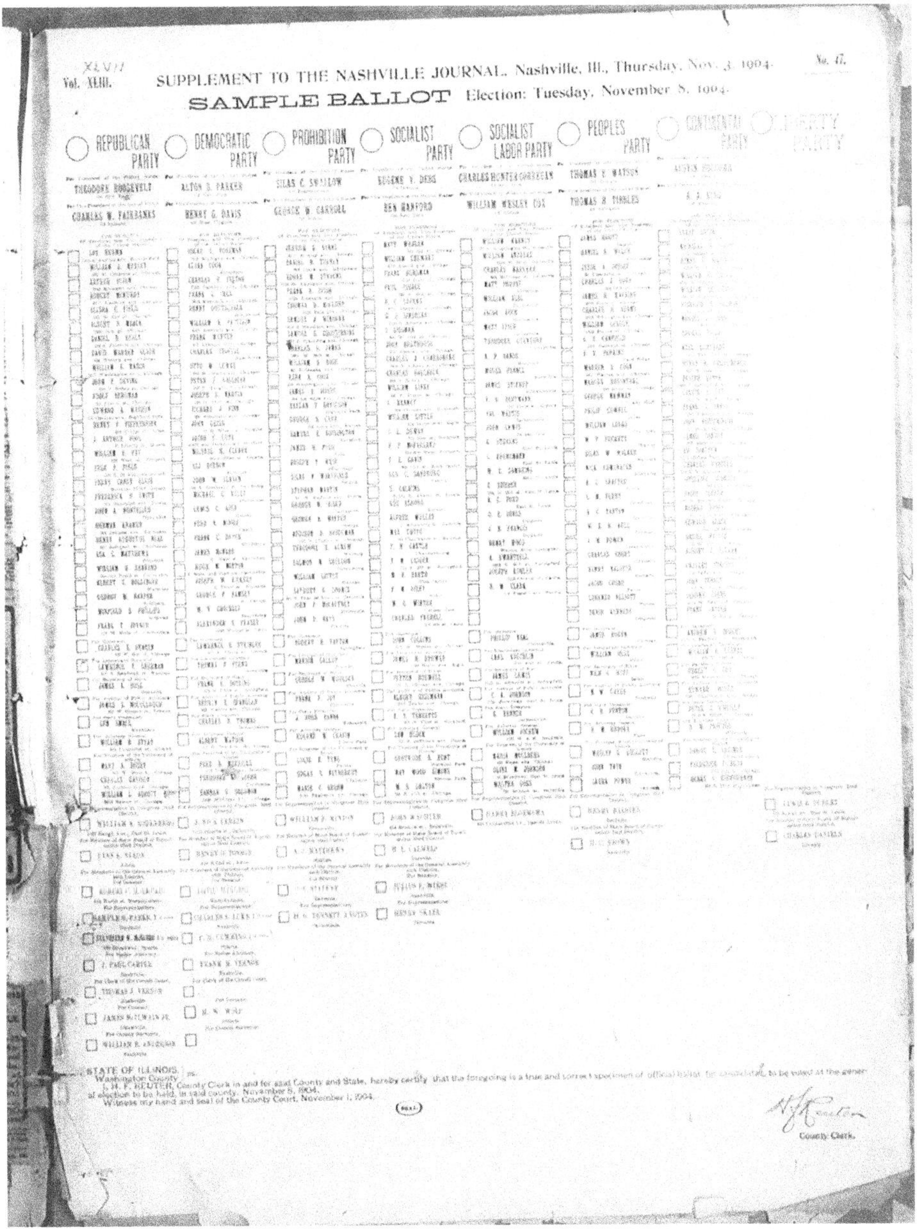

Vol. XLIII. SUPPLEMENT TO THE NASHVILLE JOURNAL, Nashville, Ill., Thursday, Nov. 3, 1904. No. 47.

SAMPLE BALLOT Election: Tuesday, November 8, 1904.

REPUBLICAN PARTY — THEODORE ROOSEVELT — CHARLES W. FAIRBANKS

DEMOCRATIC PARTY — ALTON B. PARKER — HENRY G. DAVIS

PROHIBITION PARTY — SILAS C. SWALLOW — GEORGE W. CARROLL

SOCIALIST PARTY — EUGENE V. DEBS — BEN HANFORD

SOCIALIST LABOR PARTY — CHARLES HUNTER CORREGAN — WILLIAM WESLEY COX

PEOPLES PARTY — THOMAS E. WATSON — THOMAS H. TIBBLES

CONTINENTAL PARTY — AUSTIN HOLCOMB — A. J. KING

LIBERTY PARTY

STATE OF ILLINOIS, Washington County, ss.
I, H. F. REUTER, County Clerk in and for said County and State, hereby certify that the foregoing is a true and correct specimen of official ballot … to be voted at the general election to be held in said county, November 8, 1904.
Witness my hand and seal of the County Court, November 1, 1904.

County Clerk.

Figure C.10 1904 Illinois Ballot

Sample Certificate of Ascertainment: New Mexico 2016[68]

The Certificate of Ascertainment credentials the Presidential Electors. It is created by the state to authenticate the selection of the electors, and it is attached to the paperwork which the electors complete concerning how they voted, which is sent to Congress for counting.

The Certificate of Ascertainment shows the true election result. Since New Mexico used a mandatory straight ticket in 2016, the vote counts for each Elector are grouped. When voters cast mixed elector ballots, the vote counts will be shown for the individual electors, since they will differ.

---

[68] "State of New Mexico, Office of the Governor, Certificate of Ascertainment," https://www.archives.gov/files/electoral-college/2016/ascertainment-new-mexico.pdf, accessed September 19, 2020.

STATE OF NEW MEXICO
OFFICE OF THE GOVERNOR
CERTIFICATE OF ASCERTAINMENT

I, **Susana Martinez, Governor of the State of New Mexico,** certify that the following are the official total votes received by the presidential electors whose names of party nominees for President and Vice-President of the United States, respectively, appeared on the General Election ballot of November 8, 2016, which names and votes were certified by the **New Mexico State Canvassing Board** on November 29, 2016:

ELECTORS	PARTY	CANDIDATES	VOTES
Robert Martinez Jo Mitchell Ed Cassidy Charles Moran Marge Teague	Republican	Donald J. Trump Michael R. Pence	319,666
Roxanne Allen John Padilla Edward Paul Torres Lorraine Spradling Noyola Archibeque	Democratic	Hillary Rodham Clinton Timothy Michael Kaine	385,234
Joel M. Gallegos Christopher Robert Banks Marissa Elyse Sanchez Benjamin T. Imbus Candice Jeannette Yanez	Party for Socialism and Liberation	Gloria La Riva Dennis Banks	1,184
Marty Swinney Elizabeth Honce Sherry Heim Allen Cogbill Mike Blessing	Libertarian	Gary Johnson Bill Weld	74,541
Aaron D. Abell Charleen Bishop Robert M. Bowen Nicholas Lomas Robert McKay	Constitution	Darrell Castle Scott Bradley	1,514
Sky Tallman Michal Mudd Richard Yost Peter Rogers Zacary Wilson	Green	Jill Stein Ajamu Baraka	9,879
Jennifer Ag Lisa Romeo Vincent Sanchez Priscilla Augustine Nathan Hoffman	American Delta	"Rocky" Roque De La Fuente Michael Steinberg	475
Raymond Byrne Connie Harrington Matt Jernigan Jacqueline Farnsworth David Knapp	Better for America	Evan McMullin Nathan Johnson	5,825

GIVEN UNDER MY HAND and the Great Seal of the State of New Mexico in the City of Santa Fe, at the State Capitol, on the 29th day of November, 2016.

SUSANA MARTINEZ, GOVERNOR

ATTEST:

BRAD WINTER, SECRETARY OF STATE

Figure D.1 2016 New Mexico Certificate of Ascertainment

Note on Timing

I would have loved to have published this book two years ago. But two years ago, I didn't fully understand this matter. This book isn't about any one particular election, but hopefully it provides a path forward.

Acknowledgments

Many thanks to Richard Winger at *Ballot Access News* (http://ballot-access. org/). *Ballot Access News* chronicles the hidden struggle of democracy where major-party interests keep smaller parties and independents off of our ballots, and in doing so, limit democracy to their own needs. The fight for ballot access plays quietly at the very edge of our democracy. This book would not have been possible without his insights and statistics. His knowledge of American elections is breathtaking and far exceeds that of this author.